All the Microsoft Tools You Need to Transform Your Classroom

75 Ideas for using Microsoft Office 365 for Education

By Matthew Nickerson
Foreword by Mike Tholfsen

All the Microsoft Tools You Need to Transform Your Classroom is an independent publication and is neither affiliated with, nor authorized, sponsored, or approved by Microsoft Corporation.

Contents

Introduction 6
Microsoft Office and Office 365 11
Windows 10 14
Microsoft Word 15
PowerPoint 16
Microsoft Forms 17
Sway 18
Immersive Reader 19
Stream 20
Flipgrid 21
Skype in the Classroom 22
OneNote 23
OneNote Class Notebook 24
Microsoft Teams 25
Planner 26
Bookings 27
Windows 10 28
   1 Sync OneDrive (Windows 10 29
   2 Customize your Start Menu 30
   3 Windows 10 Task View 31
   4 Alt Keys to show single-key shortcuts 33
Microsoft Word 34
   5 Headings 35
   6 Styles 36
   7 Dictate 37
   9 Drawing Canvas 39
   10 Help- Show Training 40
PowerPoint 41
   11 Templates 42
   12 Backgrounds 43
   13 Comics/Storyboards with Pixton 44
   14 Word Cloud 45
   15 Captions 46

16 Translate Captions 47
17 Remove Background 48
18 Reuse Slides 49
19 Trading Card Template 50
20 Slide Recorder 51
21 Advanced Slide Recorder 52
22 Screen Recorder 53
23 Growth with Morph 54
24 Non-linear Zoom 56

Microsoft Forms 58
27 Sections in Quizzes 61
28 Branching in Surveys 63
29 Branching in Quizzes 65

Microsoft Sway 67
33 Topics 71
34 WordSway 73

Immersive Reader 75
35 Read Aloud 76
36 Line Focus 77
37 Background Color 78

Microsoft Stream 79
38 Upload Tutorials 80
39 Upload Student Projects 81
40 Captioning 82

Flipgrid 83
41 Video Responses 84
42 Advice for Next Year's Students 85
43. Field Trips 86
44. Sales Pitch 87
45 Book Reviews 88

Skype in the Classroom 89
46. Mystery Skype 90
47. Virtual Field Trip 91
48 Author Skype 92

OneNote 93
49. Digital Portfolio 94

- 50. Print to OneNote 95
- 51 Math Tools 96
- 52 Ink Replay 97
- 53. Embed Sway 98
- 55. Embed Stream 100
- 56 Office Lens to OneNote 101
- 57 Insert Forms Quiz 103

OneNote Class Notebook 105
- 58 Distribute Pages 106
- 59 Distribute Assignments 107
- 60 Teacher Only Section 108
- 61 Distribute to Students from the Teacher-Only Section 109
- 62 Inking Feedback 110
- 63 Audio Feedback 111

Microsoft Teams 112
- 64 Use Teams to Communicate 113
- 65 Conversation 114
- 66 Video Meeting 115
- 67 Tabs 116
- 68 @ Mentions 117
- 69 Praise 118
- 70 Assignments in Teams 119
- 71 Reuse Assignments and Quizzes 120
- 72 Different Due Dates and Deadlines 121

Planner 122
- 73 Track Long-term Projects 123
- 74 Event Planning 124

Bookings 125
- 75 Schedule Meetings 126

Conclusion 127

Foreword

Matthew Nickerson is one of those rare educators that is able to seamlessly synthesize good pedagogy, creativity, and technology into one nice swirl. I first met Matt on Twitter, and then IRL (in real life) at a conference, and we've stayed in contact ever since. Matt's new book "All the Microsoft Tools You Need to Transform Your Classroom: 75 Ideas for using Microsoft Office 365 for Education" does an amazing job of taking many different classroom ideas and scenarios and gives educators useful and practical tips of how to fuse technology with each scenario in innovative ways.

This book serves as a nice guide to the modern world of the Microsoft Education tools you can use in the classroom and shows the diversity of things that educators can do today. As Matt's Twitter profile indicates, this dad of eight kids covers more products in this book than he has children! The best part is that these tips are practical, useful, and will immediately help any educator, whether new or experienced, in the classroom.

Mike Tholfsen
Product Manager
Microsoft Education
@mtholfsen

INTRODUCTION

In the beginning, there was Word, and Word was with PowerPoint, and they "Exceled". They were collectively known as Microsoft Office. Maybe you also used Publisher and Access. Remember how you used to buy a new version every few years and install it from some discs, first CD-ROMs then DVD-ROMs? We have come a long way since then.

Of course, now there are web versions as well as desktop versions, we've moved from programs to apps, and updates just roll out automatically through your subscription service. We will look at some of those differences, including how some of the desktop and web versions differ, but first, let's answer the question, "Why Microsoft"?

I spent the first 20 plus years of my career in Special Education, before moving into the world of Instructional Technology (the other IT!) Just after I made that switch, Google Apps for Education, then Google Classroom, took education by storm, taking advantage of, among other things, the perfectly timed emergence of the Chromebook, which now accounts for over half the devices in K-12 education nationwide. (I say perfectly timed, because, I remember when netbooks first came out, and how they were largely dismissed as being slightly less expensive than the cheapest laptops, but significantly less useful. Chrome OS changed that, but so did the timing of the industry moving toward online services.)

I, too, jumped on the Google bandwagon. But we have a pretty small office, and once two of the four full-time trainers had multiple Google certifications, I wondered if we needed a third. In the meantime, I was trying to figure out this OneNote thing, and going about it all wrong.

Then Immersive Reader happened. As I said, I spent over two decades in Special Education, so this amazing accessibility tool caught my attention and my imagination. Like many of the cool new features in the Microsoft realm, Immersive Reader began in OneNote. I began to understand how OneNote works even as Microsoft continued adding new tools and features there.

The organization of a OneNote digital binder is unparalleled in educational technology, and that in itself makes it an extraordinary accessibility tool, but it became the first Ed Tech tool I was aware of to have both speech to text (dictation) and text to speech (read aloud) in the same app. Then came the translation tools and the math tools, and by this time I realized that a big part of Microsoft's push into the education sector is inclusion. Immersive Reader itself is probably the premier example of Universal Design for Learning. Everything in I.R. is universally available to all users, and it is completely granular- each user can turn on or off any given feature. Use it if and when you need it and turn it off if and when you don't. Accessibility is one of the hallmarks of Microsoft's education technology offerings.

The other hallmark is the integration and complexity. I see them as one, but we will examine them separately.

By integration, consider one of the big differences in how Microsoft and Google leverage their productivity tools. Google's library of add-ins and extensions is massive, because they encourage development by third parties. So, you have several extensions or add-ins that will translate or read aloud. But they are from different developers, so they don't necessarily work together. Microsoft mostly does their own stuff. This is in large part due to much stricter security standards, but the result is tighter integration. As an example, there is a Math tool in One Note that shows the solution to an equation. And graphs it. And shows the solution steps. Sometimes two different ways. But there is also Immersive Reader, so you can open the solution steps in Immersive Reader to hear the steps read aloud (and a dozen other features to assist in reading.) But Immersive Reader can also translate into over 50 different languages. So, you write a single equation and listen to/ read along to the solution steps in Latin American Spanish, because all these features integrate.

By complexity, I mean that Google keeps things very simple, easy to learn, easy to use. That's partially because there are fewer features. I often say the way things stack up, in terms of features, is that Word online is the most basic, Google Docs has more features than Word Online, but the desktop version of Word remains the undisputed heavyweight champion. The same holds true for PowerPoint and Excel. There are far more features in PowerPoint on the desktop, far more ways you can use it, even things you can create in PowerPoint that can't even run in Google Slides. But the biggest difference in terms of simplicity and complexity is probably between Google Classroom and Microsoft Teams.

Classroom is like a pair of pliers- just pick them up and squeeze, so easy, so simple. It's a lot more work up front to find the right size socket and put that socket on the right-size ratchet. But boy, once you do, what a difference it makes to use the right tool for the job. Teams, especially if you take advantage of Class Notebook, is far more complex than Classroom. Complex means more complicated to learn, but also more useful. Teams is also more integrated; within Teams you have the communication tools of Outlook and Skype, the storage of OneDrive and OneNote, the organization tools of OneNote and Outlook, with SIS and gradebook integration for rostering and grading, a shared Team drive, integration with Planner and third-party apps like Nearpod.

Another example is Google Drawings. Wait, you say, Microsoft doesn't even have a comparable program. No, it doesn't. It doesn't need to. What Google created a separate app for is already built into PowerPoint, Word and OneNote. (Google has greatly improved the integration of Drawings into Docs and Slides recently.)

So, the way I see it, Microsoft's strategy to win back the education market that Google has such a big head start into, is two-fold. First, a strong emphasis on accessibility, and secondly, offering a more integrated and comprehensive solution. By the way, the exception to the pecking order above is that Microsoft, fully realizing that over half the devices in K-12 education are currently

Chromebooks, has put all their accessibility features into the web version of their apps so they are available to everyone, to the point that Immersive Reader has more features in Word Online than in Word Desktop.

One other consideration is market share. Google currently owns the education market, but Microsoft still has a near-monopoly of Fortune 500 companies and all levels of government. That's not likely to change anytime soon, both because of the security issues and the costs of switching platforms. So, the question can be asked, are we doing a disservice to students by not preparing them for a Microsoft Office dominated post K-12 world? As an example, when my son started high school, at Back to School Night, the Guidance Counselors met with parents of 9th graders and shared many tips. We live very close to NSA (so I can't tell you where I live) and many students in our county get internships there that can turn into a very good career right out of high school. The Guidance Counselor told us if we want our children to be considered for one of those internships, they need to have two years of Google Office classes. I'm kidding. There's no such thing. It has to be Microsoft Office training.

So that's how I became "the Microsoft Guy" in our district.
Now, let's take a brief look at all these tools that you can find in the Microsoft Universe.

MICROSOFT OFFICE AND OFFICE 365

The title of this book was originally going to be somewhat misleading. 365 Ideas for using Office 365 in the Classroom, Volume One. First, Volume one, along with the subtitle, was intended to let you know up front that this does not contain all 365 ideas. Secondly, Office 365, strictly speaking, refers to the online versions of tools like PowerPoint and Word. However, some of what is contained here is actually part of the desktop versions of Word and especially PowerPoint.

The icons  and

throughout the book indicate which version(s) have the feature being addressed, at the time of publication, since Microsoft is continually adding additional features to additional versions all the time. For example, our first tool, OneDrive, which is cloud storage, is obviously web-based. You might be surprised to learn, however, that you can also access it on your desktop. You can even use it like any other Drive (C:, D:, etc.) on your desktop once you sync OneDrive to your device, so it gets both icons.

OneDrive

OneDrive is first and foremost, cloud-based storage. Think of it as the big thumb drive (USB drive) in the sky. Except that you can't accidently forget it or leave it somewhere. You can store any kind of file whatsoever in OneDrive- documents, spreadsheets, videos, SMART Notebook lessons, audio clips, Minecraft worlds, even urls (web site addresses). As long as you have an internet connection, you can access whatever you put, or want to put, in OneDrive. One Drive gives users 1 TB of space. That's more than my entire high school had for server space just a couple years ago. It is also possible to access your OneDrive content on your desktop even if the internet is out, if you sync your OneDrive to your desktop. Syncing also allows you to move things in and out of OneDrive to the other drives on your computer, or your desktop, just by clicking and dragging.

One Drive is also a hub for all of the other Office 365 Applications. When you are logged into OneDrive, you are logged into Office 365, and in the top left corner of your screen is the "App Launcher", or waffle. Before you click on the App Launcher it is a white waffle, and when you click on it, it turns into a black waffle.

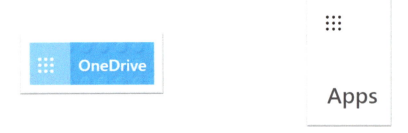

The app launcher shows the most commonly used apps in Office 365, like Word, PowerPoint, Excel and OneNote. It also uses a bit of Artificial Intelligence

(AI) to populate some more applications based on which ones you use most often. This means the apps you see will be different from what I see, and yours can change over time with your discovery and usage of different Office 365 apps. So, you might not see Stream now, but if you start using it, it will be added to your list. There are more apps than what you see when you just click the App Launcher. If you click on "All apps" at the bottom of the list, you will see the entire list, alphabetically. There is usually more than one way to get to things in Office 365, so you can also get to the list of all apps by clicking on Office 365 at the top and then All apps on that page (but that's two clicks instead of one!)

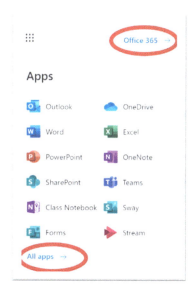

We will explore many of these apps soon, but first let's point out some features of Windows 10 you may not be aware of.

WINDOWS 10

Windows 10 has Cortana built in. Cortana is the lesser-known cousin of Alexa and Siri, a digital voice assistant. Cortana is not labelled in Windows 10, but it is what powers the search box at the bottom left corner of your screen. You can specify your search by type of content, or just start typing and search all content for your key words.

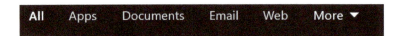

Right next to the Cortana search box is the Windows icon, which is where you click to access the Windows Start menu.

This opens an alphabetical list of all the apps and programs you have installed on this device. At the top of the list are items you have recently installed.

To the right are "Tiles", which you can rearrange, add or delete, resize, and group, then name and rearrange the groups. In addition to adding tiles here, you can also add apps to the Task Bar (the area at the bottom of your screen), so they are always visible no matter what else you have open on your desktop.

MICROSOFT WORD

Microsoft Word is of course Word Processing software, and the Microsoft Office tool most familiar to most users. There is both a desktop version and also a web version. As we noted in the introduction, the desktop version is the fully featured version, and the web version is more basic, except that the web version has the full features of Immersive Reader, and at this time the desktop version of Word is playing catchup. You are probably most familiar with Word for writing papers, but there are many templates available in Word for formats like newsletters, brochures and flyers. You can draw in Word and insert videos and tables; you can dictate in Word and use read aloud and other accessibility tools.

POWERPOINT

PowerPoint is capable of so much more than just presentations, and PowerPoint presentations can do so much more than slides and animations. However, slideshows were the first and still are the primary use for PowerPoint. The differences between the capabilities of the desktop and web versions are probably more pronounced for PowerPoint than for any other Microsoft Office tool except OneNote. Only the desktop version has the slide recorder and the screen recorder, far more educational templates, and cool features like Morph, which is a slide transition that automatically animates changes in size, shape, location and color of objects. Both versions have Zoom, which is handy for anything from a clickable Table of Contents, to Choose Your Own Adventure style stories to nonlinear slideshows. There are also really powerful shape and drawing tools and a built-in background removing tool for images.

MICROSOFT FORMS

Microsoft Forms is completely online. There is no "desktop version", although you can certainly embed a Form into a desktop app like Word or OneNote once you have created it online.

Forms is a tool for creating surveys and polls as well as quizzes. There are about eight question types in Forms, and quizzes have answer keys. Some question types can automatically grade responses. You can now add sections to Forms, which are text boxes without questions. This means you can add a reading passage that will stay visible as students answer the questions in that section. When it is time to answer questions about another reading selection, create another section. Forms also supports conditional responses, and they are really easy to set up. That means, for example, if you choose answer A for question #1, you are sent to question #2, but if you choose B you can be sent to question #4, and if you choose C you can be sent to question #6. This now works in conjunction with Sections as well.

You can see the results right inside of Forms as responses are submitted or view them in an Excel spreadsheet. You can also take that Form and embed it into different websites or apps.

SWAY

When I first heard about Sway, it seemed like a New Coke moment. Like the Google Slides people had to be snickering like Pepsi did in the 80's. "What's wrong with PowerPoint that you had to create a whole new presentation tool?" Or is Sway a website creation tool? It's a little bit of both. Every Sway has its own url, and they can scroll horizontally or vertically, so they look and feel like a website, but not in the traditional sense on menu on the left, click to go to different pages. It really is for presentations, but also for your newsletters or your syllabus. I like making Sways and embedding them in OneNote or Nearpod, but my favorite use for Sway is for students to make them. Sway is great at getting students to focus on content and not spend all their time on pictures, fonts and colors. Sway uses AI for the design work, so students really do just work on the content.

IMMERSIVE READER

Immersive Reader began its life in OneNote, but it is so powerful and so effective that you can find it across Microsoft Office and beyond. It recently found its way into Minecraft, and now Microsoft has enabled third party apps to add the tool, so you will find Immersive Reader in places like Buncee, Nearpod and Wakelet, which, while they work well with Office 365, are not Microsoft products.

So, what is Immersive Reader? A very Universal Design for Learning (UDL) friendly suite of reading tools to make text accessible for everyone, even non-English speakers.

Immersive Reader has text to speech (read aloud), tools to change font size and spacing, change the background color, only show 1, 3 or 5 lines of text at a time, break words into syllables, color-code parts of speech, a picture dictionary, and it translates words or entire documents into over 50 languages, which can all be read aloud.

Immersive Reader is a comprehensive suite of reading tools, with very granular controls. That means every single user has all of the tools available, and each can be turned on when needed by the individual and turned off when it is not. Most features also have multiple increments or settings for further personalization.

STREAM

I often describe Stream as your organization's own in-house YouTube. Videos you and your students upload to Stream can only be seen by people in your organization (district) and can be set more restrictive than that- just the class or just the teacher. Stream automatically creates closed captioning and a transcript that is editable and also features as a "zoom to this part of the video". Stream videos and channels have unique urls so they can be shared by posting or embedding in Teams, OneNote, OneDrive or other non-Microsoft sites like Nearpod or even Google Classroom. Again, Stream is designed to work within a district or organization, so if you post the link outside of Office 365, users will have to be logged into your district's Office 365 account to see the video.

FLIPGRID

Flipgrid is a very different video tool. Flipgrid is also completely online, and is its own website. Microsoft bought Flipgrid in 2018, and promptly gave refunds to anyone that had paid for the premium version, while giving all users access to those premium features.

At its heart, Flipgrid, well, flips the conversation to a video platform. Think of it like Instagram for the classroom. The teacher posts a question, ideally in a short video prompt, but it can be written instead. Students respond to the question by recording a short video reply. Usually everyone in the class can see each other's responses, because the purpose is to use videos to have a group discussion, but you can change the settings so only the teacher can see the submissions. Otherwise, students can reply to one another, give feedback and ask deeper follow-up questions of each other.

Flipgrid has many other features that add to the video creation experience and creative teachers have learned to use Flipgrid for scavenger hunts and on field trips in addition to simply being an alternate option for responding for students that prefer not to or have difficulty responding in writing.

SKYPE IN THE CLASSROOM

Skype is a tool for video conferencing. You can connect with a teacher down the hall, in another building in your district, in another state, another time zone, another country or another continent. You can connect with a class that speaks the same language or a different one. You can also connect with an author, an expert in their field or one of the creators of Minecraft. You can take students on a virtual field trip to a museum or national park or even under the ocean. What's different about doing this through Skype in the classroom is that, unlike some of my other favorites like Nearpod virtual tours or Google Earth or Expeditions, is that it is not a pre-recorded, static tour. It's a live, real time, two-way interaction with other real, live people.

There are other video conferencing tools out there, but nothing has the library of lesson plans, experts and fellow-educators and the existing infrastructure that makes it easy to make the connections that Skype in the Classroom has. All you need is a computer with an internet connection and a webcam to connect your students with anyone in the world.

ONENOTE

OneNote started life as a digital binder system. A single notebook had sections, which visually looked like tabs, and pages within these sections. OneNote was and is incredibly useful for organization. I used to say you don't create in OneNote- you create in other places and store and organize in OneNote. That's only partially true now. You can create plenty in OneNote. OneNote is still great for things like gathering research, but I compose all the time in OneNote. OneNote has amazing drawing tools that can also be used to annotate text and label diagrams. OneNote allows you to record audio while you take notes, and the audio notes are broken into little segments attached to wherever you are writing or typing on the page. You can solve math problems in OneNote and see and hear the steps to solve the problem, in multiple languages, and then OneNote can automatically create a practice quiz, complete with answer key, from that one math problem. OneNote is a little unusual in that there are not two, but three versions. There is OneNote Online and the OneNote Windows 10 app, but also an older OneNote 2016 desktop program. This one used to have all the best features, but all the newer features have been added to the windows 10 app, while features that only exist in OneNote 2016 are continually being added to the Windows 10 app. Personally, I switched over to the app as my primary version about a year ago and only open 2016 when I need a specific feature that doesn't work in the app yet.

ONENOTE CLASS NOTEBOOK

OneNote Class Notebook is essentially three (or four) OneNote notebooks in one. There is a collaborate section, which everyone in the class has access to for reading and writing, meaning everyone can edit anything in that section. There is also a Content Library section, which is read only for students and only the teacher can edit that content, so it's great for not only beginning of the year items like a syllabus, but also daily instructional materials like digital handouts. Each student also has their own section group that only they and the teacher can see and edit. The teacher sets up what sections are within that notebook, like warmups, classwork, notes, homework, or units in a course. The teacher has a tab for each student on the class.

There is an optional fourth section called Teacher Only. This is a great place for staging materials. Teachers can plan here, or even place or build their entire curriculum here, which nobody else can see. Then, as the time comes to use that content, they can copy to the content library or distribute a copy to each students' section. Class Notebook can be connected to Microsoft Teams or an LMS so grades on assignments can be automatically transferred. Of course, all the features in OneNote are true for OneNote Class Notebook as well.

MICROSOFT TEAMS

Microsoft Teams is the digital hub for all things Office 365. Teams was originally designed for businesses. Initially Microsoft's answer to Google Classroom was going to be a project called, very unoriginally, Microsoft Classroom. Classroom was scrapped in part because it wasn't all that good, but also because they realized that already had a vastly superior tool in Teams. Because Teams was designed for business, and for transparency, you could create different channels in a Team, but everybody in ne channel could still see everything in the other channels. Teams is where the marketing division, the engineering team, and the sales group could all communicate with each other. So, while the sales content was housed in the Sales channel, marketing and engineering could see it all. Again, transparency. This works great in the classroom when the channels are unit 1 and unit 2, but not so well when you create additional channels for small groups. At the time of writing, Microsoft is promising to roll out private channels in the next few weeks, so by the time you are reading this, hopefully you will have that ability.

Teams has Skype for Business built in, so you can have scheduled or impromptu video or audio meetings, complete with screen-sharing. Outlook calendars are built into Teams. Teams has a conversation tab for the whole class to post and respond to each other, and also has private chats that your district may turn off for students. Posts don't have to be just text. You can add attachments, emojis, stickers, weblinks and GIFs to your posts and replies. Your

OneDrive is available in the far-left column, but the Team has its own 1 TB of group storage available in each channel. There are tabs at the top to easily access the conversation space, the File storage space, and other tabs can be added and deleted as needed, so that can be used for things your class always needs access to, but also today's materials, which can be replaced daily.

PLANNER

Planner is specifically available in Office 365 only, meaning there is no desktop version of it.

Planner is for task management, either for an individual or groups. I have used Planner individually to track the steps I needed to replace my deck one summer and collaboratively to plan a teacher conference. You can create as many columns (Planner calls the buckets) as needed, like "To Do', "Assigned", "In Progress", and "Completed", or whatever you need. You can add people ahead of time, or add them as you assign tasks to them. There are multiple views of progress, including a calendar and graphs.

BOOKINGS

Bookings is also strictly an online tool, found in the App Launcher in Office 365. Like Planner, most likely you will have to click on "All apps" to find this one.

Bookings is a scheduling tool, which, for classroom teachers may only be needed for parent conference time, but if you do any conferencing with students you may have other uses for. Bookings looks at your Outlook calendar to find your availability, and you can set different blocks of time people can schedule with you. If your Outlook calendar shows 45 minutes of availability, they will see one block available for a 30minute meeting, but no availability for a one-hour meeting. Bookings can also be used for checking out rooms or resources, and they will each have their own outlook calendar created.

Those are the tools discussed in this volume, so now we can dig in and start seeing ways they can be used.

WINDOWS 10

1 Sync OneDrive (Windows 10)

When you sync your OneDrive to your windows device, OneDrive is listed among the rest of your folders. In other words, you don't have to open a web browser to access your files stored in OneDrive. But that's just the beginning of the benefits. When you are downloading something from the internet, you can choose to save it directly to OneDrive as well. This means you don't have to download to your device, and then upload from your device to OneDrive, saving you time and eliminating needless steps. It works the other way around as well- you can open documents, presentations and files from OneDrive directly from you Windows Explorer (Files) menu.

Note that even though this is my personal device, I can sync personal and work OneDrive accounts.

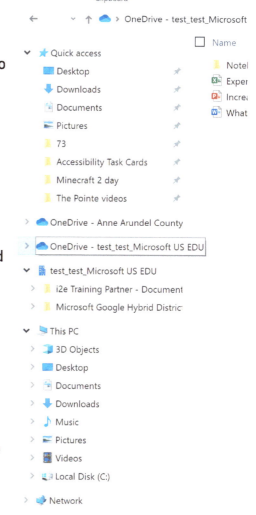

2 Customize your Start Menu

When you click on the Windows 10 icon in the bottom left corner of your screen your Start Menu opens. If you drag an app from this list to the right or right-click on an app and choose "Pin to Start", that app's tile gets added to the area to the right. That's because this entire area is your start menu. You can then click and drag the tile where you want it.

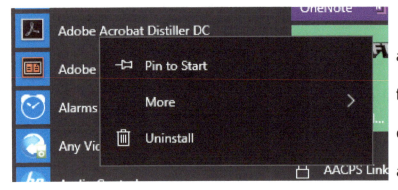

That's easy access for apps you use regularly, but for an app you use daily, you can go a step further and add it to your task bar. That's the area at the bottom of your screen.

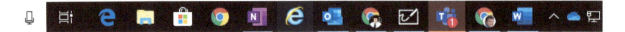

You can add an icon to your task bar by right-clicking on the icon in the Start Menu and choosing "More", then "Pin to Taskbar".

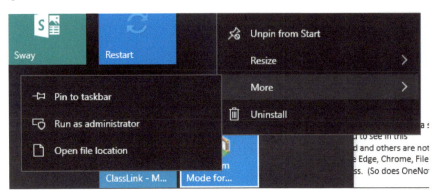

3 Windows 10 Task View

There are several other settings you can customize on your Taskbar.

If you right-click in some open space (not on an icon) on your Taskbar, you will get a box that looks something like this. Whatever has a check mark next to it is activated, and whatever does not, isn't. Click on anything that doesn't have a check mark to activate it and see what it gives you. Make sure Show Task View button has a check mark.

The Task View button shows all your open windows in thumbnails. I'm using two screens, so it even separates my windows by screen. Notice in the top left corner of each screen that I currently have desktop 1 and Desktop 2. If you are not familiar with this, it does NOT mean monitor screens 1 and 2. It is two separate workspaces for multitasking. In my world, I have started using it to have one desktop for my daily work, and a second for

> You may prefer to use it to have work on one Desktop and personal things on a different desktop, and you can switch between them easily.

presenting. I don't have to close everything to "hide" it, just open whatever materials I need when presenting in another desktop that's very clean and only has what I need for that presentation on it.

I also highly recommend turning on the Desktop toolbar. You can add it under *Toobars.* This will place the word "Desktop" in your taskbar with a double-carat next to it.

Click on the double-carat and a list of all the folders and files on your desktop will pop-up. Now you can open anything on your desktop without having to close or minimize all your open windows!

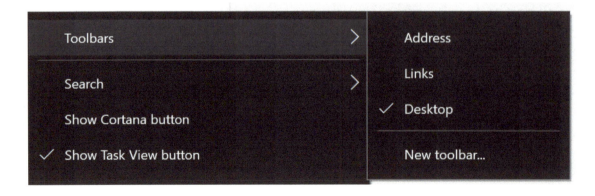

4 Alt Keys to show single-key shortcuts

Universal Design for Learning often involves tools that were designed for someone with a disability but is found to be useful for the general public. Across all the desktop Office Suite programs (Word, Excel, PowerPoint, OneNote, etc.), when you press the Alt key, letters appear across the ribbon at the top of the screen. If you press one of those letters on your keyboard, it's like clicking on that tab, and more letters show up on anything that you can click on under that tab. For students that have a physical difficulty using a mouse, this eliminates the need to use a mouse inside the Office programs. For the rest of us, it is a convenient time saver when our hands are on the keyboard. A lot of time? No, not in one single time that you click two keys instead of reaching for the mouse, clicking, and coming back. But it adds up, especially in our modern world of "Three seconds is too long! I need it faster!"

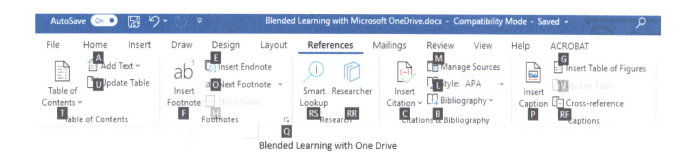

Blended Learning with One Drive

MICROSOFT WORD

5 Headings

When you turn text in a Word document into a heading, it does more than make the font larger and turn it to a prettier color. It also makes all the content between that heading and the next one collapsible. Any heading that has been collapsed will have a helpful arrow next to it, indicating that there is hidden content that you can see if you click on that arrow. When you hover over a heading that has not been collapsed, the arrow allowing you to collapse that section appears.

Utilizing Headings is an easy and attractive way to make documents more accessible by adding visual organization to documents. Documents don't have to be long for this to be helpful to students.

Skype for Business- host office h
Skype

Sway- easy to add content, co-a
images- takes care of appearanc

Forms- quizzes, surveys, questic

- Can give feedback for ri

▸ Content creation
▸ COLLABORATION
▸ Class Notebook
◢ Teams

Where to start!

-consume and create

Communicate

Collaborate

Class Notebook built in

Class calendar

> Bonus: If you also use Sway, particularly the ability to write in Word and then transform your document into a Sway webpage, Sway recognizes Headings and converts them into Heading cards instead of text cards.

6 Styles

Headings are not the only Styles in Word. Simply click and drag over the text you want to "Style", then click on the drop-down arrow next to Style (under the Home tab) and choose from Title, different levels of Headings, Quotes and different ways to emphasize your text. Microsoft Office is consistent about showing you previews. You don't have to apply a style to see what it will look like. Each style shows you a sample. Once you find a style you like, take advantage of the Format Painter to apply that style to other text.

Bonus: Did you know you can also create your own style?

Set your font, font size, font color, decide whether to add italics, bold, or underline, and you can save your Stylish creation, and it will be added to your Style gallery!

7 Dictate

Text to speech is the idea of taking typed text and reading it aloud. Dictation is the other way around- speech to text. Dictation is a tool that is available across the Office Suite of apps, as well as in Word Online and OneNote Online. This is another example of UDL. The advantages for students who have various disabilities is obvious. For students that have physical difficulty manipulating a keyboard, for students that have major issues with spelling because of dyslexia or other decoding issues, dictation can be a real game-changer. But you don't have to have a disability to benefit from dictation. Some of us just never really learned to type correctly.

Sometimes we are multitasking. Sometimes it just helps to think out loud, and Dictate can capture those thoughts. I've even used Dictate through a headset on an exercise bike. (But not in school.)

And don't forget that English is not the only language supported. You can speak in English, Chinese and Spanish and see your text appear in those languages in your document. The "preview languages" are not as refined as the five fully supported languages, meaning they will not be as accurate.

Check out dictation in PowerPoint, too!

 8 Drawing Tools

Click on the Draw tab in Word and you will find a whole suite of tools available to you and your students. Click on the drop-down arrow that appears when you hover over a pen to see different tip thicknesses, special effects and limitless color choices. You can customize this list of pens, pencils and highlighters, which travels with you across devices and even in other Office programs like OneNote and PowerPoint that also have Drawing tools.

Not only can you use Word as a place to draw freely, but if you share a poem or other text with students in a Word document, they can use these drawing tools to annotate, highlight and make notes, and color-code. Circle verbs, color-code rhyme schemes, highlight in different colors, make suggestions for peer revisions, and even label a diagram, all right within Word. No need for a separate drawing app here!

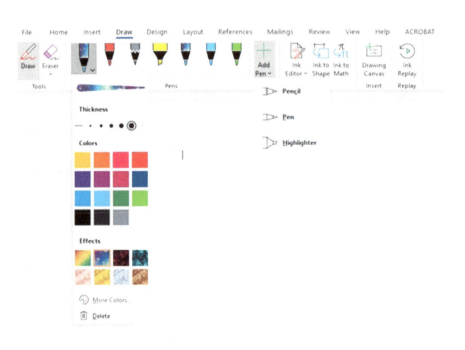

9 Drawing Canvas

A fun newer feature under the Draw tab in Word is the ability to add a drawing canvas right inside you word document. Obviously, you can use all the tools under the draw tab in the drawing canvas. But if you click into that area, and go to the Insert tab, you can insert  images, shapes, and icons, charts and even 3D models onto your drawing canvas. That means that if you insert something and then draw on it, if you click to move the shape, or picture to somewhere else in the document, the inking you highlighted, drew on or annotated moves with it. Everything on the canvas can be treated as one object. Can be, not has to be. If you want to edit something in the canvas, you can still click on that object and move, edit, resize or delete it.

Bonus Tip: This also makes it easy to place objects (like pictures) exactly where you want them, just by putting them into a canvas!

10 Help- Show Training

Everybody needs a little help sometimes and Microsoft is happy to give it. Now when you click on the Help tab in word, you can not only click on What's New to be shown new features, but you can click on show Training and access How-To training chunked into topics which are further chunked into specific skills when you click on them.

The tutorials you will find consist of written directions with plenty of screenshots showing you exactly what to click on and where it is. It's also very granular, meaning the directions are for one very specific task, including basics like "Create a document in Word", or "Save your document to OneDrive in Word", and more advanced tricks like "Insert or delete a comment" or "Collaborate on word documents with real-time co-authoring".

POWERPOINT

 11 Templates

When you open PowerPoint to create a new slideshow, do you just click on New, then "Blank Presentation" and just get into it as fast as you can? Yeah, stop that. Slow down and take a look around after you click New and resist the urge to click Blank Presentation. Right under the Search box there are suggested searches. Try clicking on Education. There are over 50 educational templates here. Some are for teachers and some are clearly designed for student use. Back to school time? Check out "Getting to know your teacher", "Student does/teacher does" or "Playground rules". Have students that need some help getting started? (Remember Vygotsky and scaffolding?) Show them "Persuasive speech outline", "Book report presentation", "Science fair presentation", or how about "Create your own colony" or "Digital time capsule".

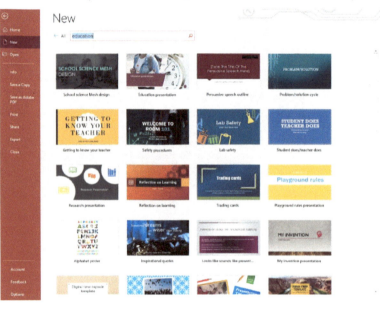

You don't have to reinvent the wheel, and neither do your students. Take advantage of the formatting that has already been done for you, and spend your time focusing on the content.

12 Backgrounds

There are a few ways to add a background to a slide in PowerPoint. Add a picture, click on Format and adjust the size to fill the page, click and drag a corner until it's fills the page on all sides and then use the cropping tool to trim it, or start with cropping. By far the easiest is to simply right-click on your slide and choose "Format background".

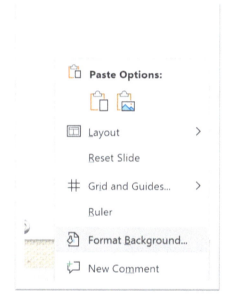

Then under "fill" choose "Picture or texture" and either "Insert" or use "ClipBoard" to paste it in. PowerPoint will automatically resize your image to fill the screen.

Notice the "Apply to all" button at the bottom. This is especially handy if you are using the background as the scene for a comic strip or story board.

> Now that Microsoft Teams allows you to upload a virtual background, create your backgrounds in PowerPoint and export them as images to use in Teams.

13 Comics/Storyboards with Pixton

Now that you have a background for your story, there's also an easy way to add characters and dialogue for you Comic Strip or Storyboard. You do NOT have to look for characters online or draw your own. It's really hard to find the same character in multiple poses anyway. If you do go that route, use Insert Shapes to add speech bubbles and thought bubbles that you can edit, resize and move around as needed.

But I recommend you try out the Pixton Add-In. (There's even a Pixton Add-in for PowerPoint Online now!) Pixton has 25 different characters, each with 25 different outfits, each with 33 full body poses AND 33 MORE upper body poses, each with and without a customizable speech bubble! That's 82,500 combinations!

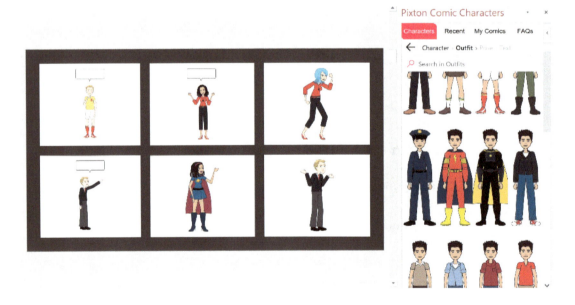

Bonus tip: Skip the speech bubbles in Pixton and add the Insert Shapes speech bubbles in PowerPoint to keep more control over the size of the font!

14 Word Cloud

Another PowerPoint Add-in is Pro Word Cloud. This allows you to create and insert Word Clouds directly within PowerPoint- no website or third party needed.

Find Add-ins under the Insert tab in the Ribbon. You can select up to 100 words of text to draw from. The more times the word is used in that text, the larger it appears in the Word Cloud. Share a blank PowerPoint with your

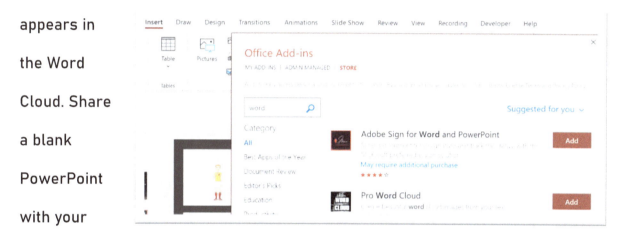

class and let them add adjectives to describe a character in a novel, then make the Word Cloud from their descriptions. Keep the Cloud on your PowerPoint slide, or just use PowerPoint to create them, and save the image to use elsewhere.

Here's a Word Cloud generated from Idea #13.

15 Captions

Add captions to your PowerPoint. What are captions? Think "Closed Captioning". PowerPoint can listen to what you say as you present and print your words on the screen in real-time. Choose to display the text at the top or bottom of the screen, on top of or just above/below your slides. Simply click on the Slide Show tab in the Ribbon and click on "Always Use Subtitles". This simple tool makes your live presentations more accessible for everyone. Who doesn't want their lesson to be accessible?

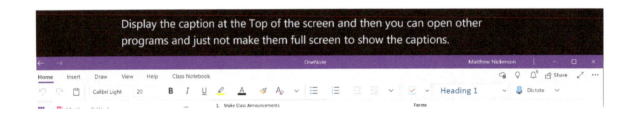

Bonus Tip: While this only works in PowerPoint, you can use PowerPoint just for the closed captioning and open other programs. Just make them less than full screen so you can still see the top of your PowerPoint screen.

 16 Translate Captions

PowerPoint live captions is multilingual. When you click on "Start Subtitles", a dialogue box pops up. You can choose which language you are speaking in, and which language you want the captions to be displayed in. PowerPoint currently recognizes speech in 13 spoken languages and can display captions in 63 different written languages.

This means that if the majority of your audience speaks a different language than you speak, you can display that language instead of your own.

This is where you can select and configure your microphone and set where the captions will appear on the screen.

Clicking "More Settings (Windows)" opens Settings where you can specify the color, size and font of captions, background color, create a textbox for them, which can even be transparent.

I use a Surface Pro, which has a great microphone, but for most devices it is very helpful, as with dictation, to use an external microphone. Microsoft uses AI to produce the captions, which is online. So, the accuracy depends on hearing you clearly. If you are translating captions, if it hears you clearly, it translates you correctly.

 17 Remove Background

Speaking of backgrounds, what if you don't want one? In your picture, that is. Earlier we showed how to make an image a background for your PowerPoint slide. What if you want to insert an image of your dog, or a tree, or a person onto that background, and you want just the dog, not a rectangle that includes the dog? One option is to search for an online image and include ".png " in your search. This should only return results with no background. But if you already have an image and it has a background, PowerPoint can remove the background for you. It uses AI initially, so if there is dramatic contrast between your dog and the background, it might be automatic. If there's less contrast, you can manually select areas to cut or areas to keep. Click on your picture and you will find

   Under the Picture Format tab.

 18 Reuse Slides

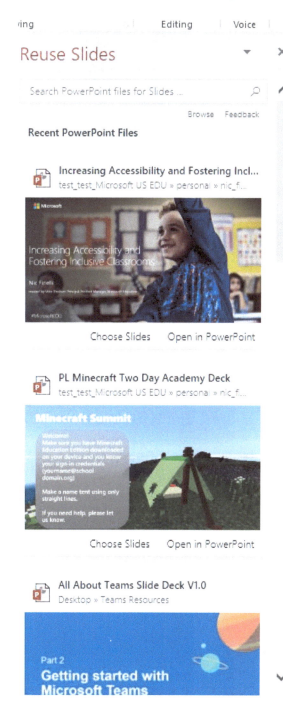

This is a handy tool I use at least weekly. If you have slides in one PowerPoint presentation that you want to add to a new presentation, "Reuse Slides" (under the Home tab on the ribbon) makes it super easy to find and insert them. A sidebar opens with PowerPoints you have opened recently, in chronological order. If the slideshow you need is one you haven't opened in a while, you can also use the Search Box. Just click on Choose Slides and the view in that sidebar will change to thumbnails of all the slides in that slideshow. A single click on any slide inserts it into your new PowerPoint.

It doesn't even have to be a slideshow you opened on this device, since your Microsoft Office account travels with you from device to device.

19 Trading Card Template

When you start a new PowerPoint presentation, don't just click through to "New blank template" without pausing to look around like you always do. There's good stuff there in the templates, including Trading Cards. Think outside the box. Sure, your students could make Trading Cards for characters in a novel or short story.

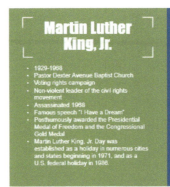

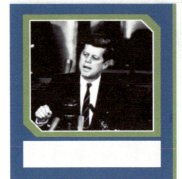
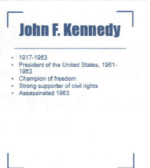

Of course, they can make cards for important historical figures. But if you think about trading card games like Pokemon, there are cards for items and even types of energy. In the same way, students could make trading cards for historical events or battles or maybe important inventions.

I've used trading cards in Biology for organisms, for scientists, and for forms of asexual reproduction. In addition, they could be made for elements or compounds.

Lest math teachers think they are the left-out-exception once again, consider trading cards for operations, fraction, decimal, percent, and geometric shapes, and for higher grade levels, algebraic properties and geometry theorems.

No matter what you teach, there's a use for Trading Cards.

 20 Slide Recorder

Use Record Slide Show, under the Recording tab on the ribbon, to record narration of your slides in any PowerPoint presentation. Basically, say whatever you would say if you were delivering the presentation live. You can record each slide individually, stop the recording, move to your next slide, think about what you want to communicate, and click record again. When you finish, you have a recorded lesson, with your slides as a visual and your voice giving instruction. Now you can distribute your lesson to students digitally, to "flip the classroom" or become a YouTube star or have your own personal version of Khan Academy.

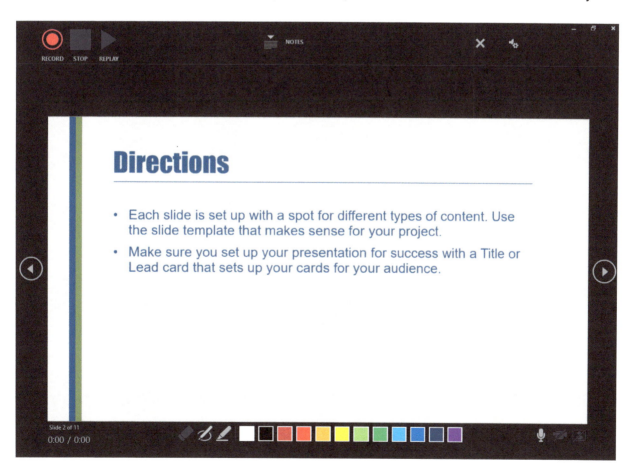

21 Advanced Slide Recorder

At the top center of the screen in Slide Recorder is a drop-down option for "Notes". These are the exact same notes that normally appear under your slides- the "speaker notes". In slide recorder they are moved to the top, center, because that is right under your webcam, so they work like a teleprompter. That's only important because in the bottom right corner of your screen, you can click to turn on/off your microphone, webcam, and preview screen. If you turn on your webcam, then viewers will see you in that corner while seeing your slides full screen and hearing you narrate. If you want to se what they will see, you can turn on the preview as well. So, if your camera is rolling, having the notes right under it is a good idea. In addition, you have a row of pens and highlighters to draw on your slides while you talk about them, so you can highlight or annotate as you go, just as you would live in front of the class.

22 Screen Recorder

The slide recorder is designed to record your PowerPoint. The screen recorder, on the other hand, is designed to use PowerPoint to record outside of PowerPoint. In other words, Screen Recorder...records your screen! Whatever is on it. You can define what part of the screen you want to capture or choose the whole screen. You can choose to narrate or not, and you can choose whether or not you want your cursor to show up in the video. (You will still see it while you record.) I use this almost daily, to record tutorials, so I always want the cursor showing. It does not record the computer audio, so you can't use this to record, for example, a YouTube video to get around your district's filter. (Actually, there is a hardware solution for that, but I'm not telling you how to circumvent your district's policies here!)

So, now that you know how to use PowerPoint to record both inside and outside of PowerPoint, where can you put these videos to share with students? (Or where can students put them to share with you?)

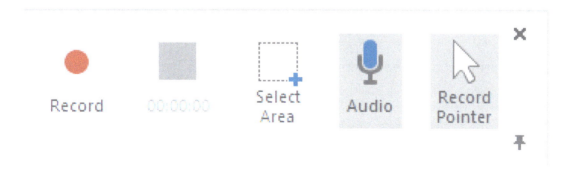

 23 Growth with Morph

Morph is a really cool transition that uses AI (Artificial Intelligence) to make items change size, color, shape and/or position as you advance from one slide to another.

Morph is hard to capture with still pictures, but the left column shows the 4 slides, and the screenshots on the right are taken during the transitions between slides 1-2 and slides 4-3 (yes, in reverse.)

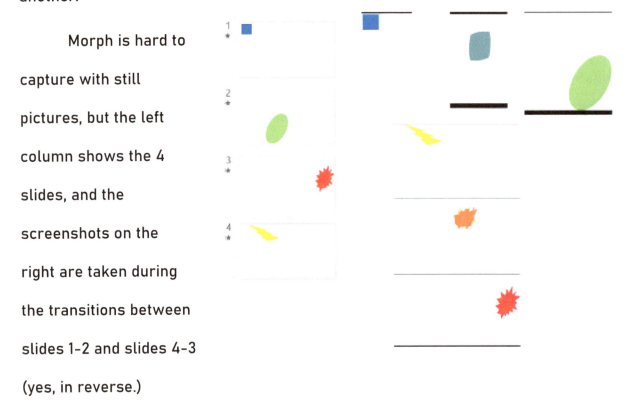

Notice that the shapes are gradually changing size, shape, color and location. Morph creates the algorithms to make these smooth changes, and to our eyes it looks like animation.

You can do this with images by placing them in one slide, duplicating the slide, then moving or resizing them in the duplicate slide. Then click on the transitions tab and choose Morph.

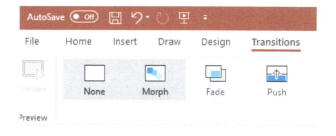

Think about how you and your students can use this easy to use visual tool in your PowerPoint presentations.

Here's a few ideas:

Morph can show transitions visually, show order, processes, movement, growth and shrinking. I've had students start with an acorn and grow it into a sapling, then a mature tree which ultimately produces more acorns! Works great with the lifecycle of a monarch butterfly as well. And, it just makes a really cool transition!

 24 Non-linear Zoom

Zoom, well, zooms from one slide to another and back again with the click of a mouse. Think of Zoom as a slick way of hyperlinking from one slide to another. When you insert a slide Zoom, thumbnails of all the slides in your presentation pops up. Simply click on the slide(s) you want to zoom to from this page. A thumbnail of the page(s) will be placed on your slide.

Zoom is really useful for any slideshow that doesn't have to be linear, whether a live presentation or sharing a slideshow for students to click through independently.

Consider a slideshow full of slides with information about **states**, or Civil War battles, or locations in **novel**, each on their own slide. Put a map on one of the first slides and place zoom links geographically to each slide.

Want to differentiate **math**? Use the Drawing tools to write the solution to a math problem. Link to slides that explain each step. Students that understand the first slide can move on. Students that need an explanation about any step can click for more information.

Science, Tech Ed or FACS teacher can start with a diagram and link to components of the diagram for details. (Ex. Parts of a cell, a sewing machine, a screenshot of Adobe Photoshop or a drill press)

In the lower image below, see if you can find slides 3, 4, and 5 in upper image!

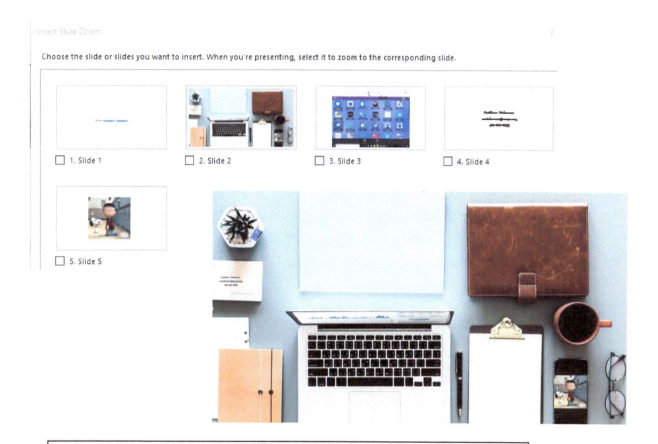

Bonus tips:

Set slides that you zoom to, to return when you click on them

Replace the thumbnail of the other slide with another image so you click on the image to go to the slide!

MICROSOFT FORMS

25 Quiz

Create, distribute and collect digital quizzes with Microsoft Forms. There are currently 8 question types, sections for adding longer text, the ability to add a reference image or video, and very simple branching- sending quiz-takers to different questions based on their answers.

You can add feedback for each answer choice. Create an answer key for Choice, multiple-answer, drop-down, rank and even short answer questions. View results right in Forms or view them in Excel.

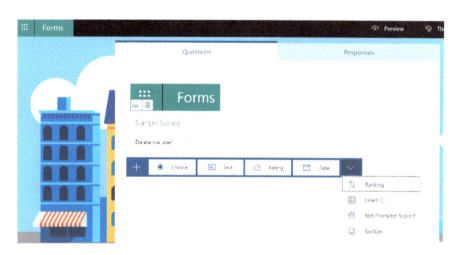

26 Survey

Create surveys and polls in Microsoft Forms. There are 8 question types, and results can be seen directly in Forms, under the "Responses" tab, or in Microsoft Excel. Create in Forms, copy the Share link and distribute the link through any digital platform- email, Blackboard/LMS, Class Notebook or Microsoft Teams. Or create a QR code or embed code without leaving Forms.

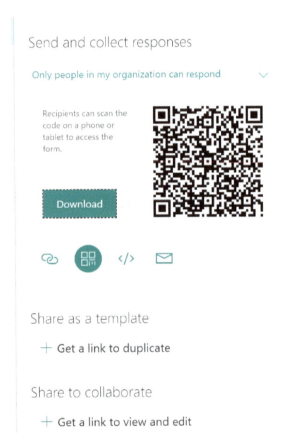

Customize the background from Microsoft's library or upload your own image. Preview at any time to see what your survey will look like on a desktop or mobile device. Optimize for mobile devices by making all Choice questions appear as Drop-down menus.

I like to use Forms for people to sign up for sessions and accounts. Anything where it is easier to copy a list of email addresses from one column than to type them all in individually!

27 Sections in Quizzes

Sections are one of the question types in Microsoft Forms, only there is no question. It is unquestionably one of the best new features in Forms, and it combines with other features in useful ways.

One use for sections is to add the material that students will use to answer a series of questions in one section. Add the related questions. The create a new section for the next material that students will answer questions about. That's easy to visualize with passages of text. Put the reading selection in a section; ask questions about that passage. Put the next passage in a new section; repeat as necessary.

However, this also works with charts, graphs, tables, and maps. Insert a diagram with numbered arrows, then add questions asking what each arrow points to, and you have a labelling activity.

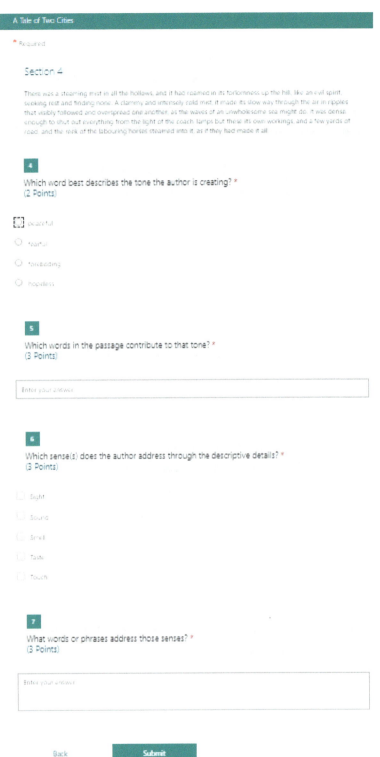

Start by adding a section. In the description box, paste in text that students will use to answer the questions in that section. Then add the questions related to that text.

The reading passage or image stays visible as long as the student is in that section. They may need to scroll up, if it is a long reading passage or there are many questions, but it will remain on *that page*- no need for a back button or multiple windows.

Sections work with branching, as you will see in the next topic, and don't forget that Forms has Immersive Reader, which is really handy with the longer text passages supported in sections.

28 Branching in Surveys

Branching is simple to set up in Microsoft Forms.

Branching sends students or respondents to different questions based on your answers. Think of it as choose your own adventure for quizzes and surveys, in the Choice question-type, including with the drop-down option.

Create your survey first. You may find it useful to write out a "map" of where you want different responses to send users if it's going to be complicated. Then, in the top right corner next to the Share button, click on the ellipses.

Next, click on Branching.

Now when you click on any question, your branching options will appear for that question. Most question types will simply have a drop-down list underneath the question to select which question to go to after answering that question. You can make any answer choice go to any question. For other question types you can send them to any question regardless of the response. That's useful for sending respondents on a little side-trip for more information, then returning them back to the main line of questioning.

Here's an example of branching in a survey.

"Did you purchase from the food truck on Monday?"

"Yes?"- give feedback about that food truck.

"No?", I can either send you on to Tuesday's food truck or to ask why you didn't purchase from Monday's truck.

This helps you when you look at the report. If I send yes answers to one question to explain, and no answers to another to explain, and then bring them both back together to move on to the next question, in my results all my "yes" explanations will be together, and all my "no" explanations will likewise be grouped.

If you have tried to do branching by sections in Google Forms, you can appreciate how much simpler this process is.

29 Branching in Quizzes

Branching is just as useful in Forms quizzes as in a survey. You can make adaptive quizzes that automatically adjust to each student's level of mastery.

In branching, multiple choice and drop-down questions allow you to send students to a question based on their response. All other question types simply allow you to choose which questions they go to after they answer that question, which is great for "round trips". Consider this:

If you answer question 1 correctly, you go on to question 2. If you answer it incorrectly, you are sent to question 11, an open-ended (text) question asking you to explain your answer. I can then send you back to question 2. Everyone is back on track together for question 2, and I got some helpful insight into the thought process of each student that missed #1.

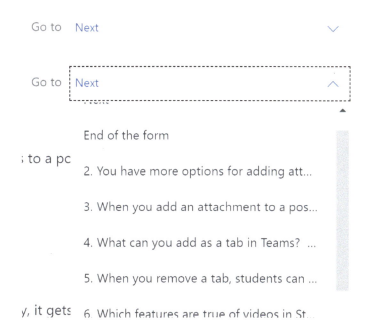

Here's another way to use branching in a quiz.

If you answer a question correctly you go to a question that is equally or more difficult. If you answer incorrectly, you go to a question that is less difficult.

Forms recently got an update to make it even easier to use branching! Now when you click on the ellipses at the bottom of a question, "Add branching" is right there.

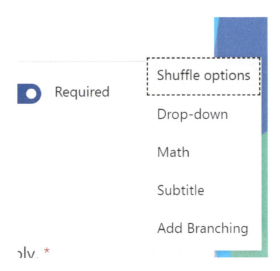

Take it to the next level:

An incorrect answer can redirect to a "section"- text without a question with more instructions for review. Since you can add a video to a question (including a section) you can have a review video placed there.

MICROSOFT SWAY

30 Student Presentations

What do your students spend most of their time doing when they create a PowerPoint or Google Slides presentation? There's a lot to love about Sway, but for me, the best part is how Sway uses A.I. for the design work, and makes students spend their time on the content! Sway was launched as an alternative presentation tool to PowerPoint, but now they openly refer to it as a website, although it's best not to think of it as a tool to create a traditional website. It can scroll vertically or horizontally, and it has its own url, but it is not intended to add pages and subpages, or to have a menu.

Instead of slides, you edit your Sway by adding "cards". There are different types of cards- headings, text, photos, photo sets, etc- that appear and behave differently depending on the type. Click "Play" at any time to get a preview of what your Sway looks like. Students can collaborate on a Sway and they can be embedded in other tools, like OneNote, Wakelet and Nearpod.

This isn't what a Sway looks like- this is just a section of the content in one sample Sway. Included below are text cards with instructions, galleries of images, and galleries of embedded videos.

31 Portfolio

One of the many uses for a Sway is as a student portfolio. That's why three of the templates (next article) in Sway are various types of portfolios. Since Sway is designed for multi-media, obviously it can showcase photos themselves, or photos of a students' creations and physical products. Students can also can gather writing samples, screen recordings or video recordings of their performance, and photos. They can upload files like Word documents, PowerPoint slideshows and Excel spreadsheets from OneDrive and/or their device. Devices, actually, since Sway is entirely web-based, they can access it from multiple devices. They can organize it with heading cards and describe their work with text cards. They can upload an image for a banner and set the Sway to scroll either horizontally or vertically. Since Sway can be set to share outside your domain even if everything else in your OneDrive can't, a Sway can be shared with a prospective employer or school. It is an incredibly visually-appealing resume'!

Once again, since Sway uses A.I. to design the presentation, your students can once again focus on creating nd gathering the content they want to showcase.

32 Templates

My other favorite thing about students making Sways is the built-in scaffolding. If you don't think your class, or maybe just some of your students, are ready to create a Sway from scratch, show them the Templates! There are currently 15 different templates to choose from. But don't worry if you can't find an exact match for the type of presentation your student wants to make. The templates just give them a target for what their final product should look like, and they replace the text and images with their own and add more cards as needed. Again, think scaffolding. It simply gives them a structure to get started.

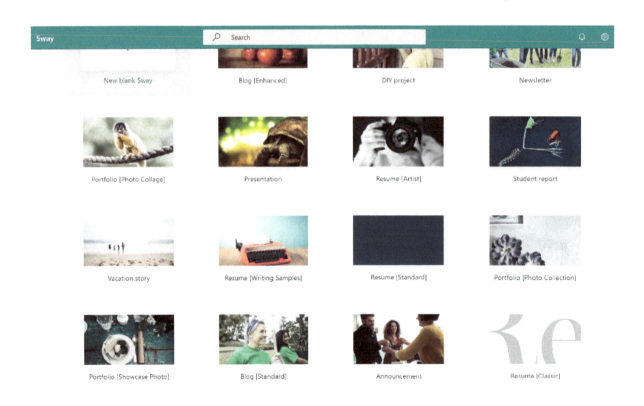

 33 Topics

For students that need even more structure than a template provides, they can *start with a topic*. When students enter a topic, it creates an outline of cards in Sway by pulling the headings from the Wikipedia article on that topic. (BTW, It *is filtered-* not *everything* in Wikipedia will yield results in a topic search in Sway.

Sway often asks a clarifying question to make sure you get the results you want. Try querying Cornell Notes. There is not an exact match, but Note-taking comes up, and Cornell Notes is one of the headings there. That's an important point, because this shows that the algorithm used to find appropriate content from your search goes deeper than just article titles.

Topics open in Edit mode. "Hints" appear throughout the Sway, as notes. You can immediately close all hints at any time by clicking on "dismiss all".

These notes function like notes in PowerPoint. They appear to the presenter, but not to the audience. In Sway, they appear in the Edit mode, to the creator, but they are nowhere in the presentation in Play mode.

Immediately after the Title card is a single (empty) text card with one paragraph of basic information about the topic in the notes section. Again, this is just for the author to see and is not part of the presentation. It's there simply to give the author a basic understanding of the topic. After that, they are just given Heading cards with topics, and, depending on the topic, one or more relevant images. Beyond that, there are just some suggestions in the notes of specific ideas to research.

What all this means is, start from a topic does not "do all the work" for a student. It simply gives them an organizational framework to do their work within. It is the next level scaffolding beyond the *templates* that some students need to organize both their research and their content.

34 WordSway

While templates and topics provide organizational scaffolding to students, you may already provide students with structure and maybe even an outline of what they need to include. In that case, you may want to use Sway completely differently. If your students are ready to jump right into creating directly within Sway, you can have them start in a more familiar medium- Microsoft Word.

Have students write their content like a traditional paper right in Word. They can type everything in a normal font, but after writing their content, they can utilize the Styles in Word to add a Title and Headings, as well as web links and images. Sway recognizes those and automatically create cards for them when students transform their Word document into a Sway presentation.

Besides starting in a more familiar program for students, teachers have some added control. Students can continue working or revising in Word until their teacher gives them the OK to move to Sway. This is especially easy if the document is shared with the teacher. (Both OneNote Class Notebook and Microsoft

Teams have the ability to distribute "copies" to each student, so the teacher already has access to all the students' Word documents for that assignment.) Keeping the students in Word until they have teacher approval ensures they continue building meaningful content and stay focused on that task and Sway becomes a carrot to work toward, and gives the students a sense of accomplishment.

In Word, Transform can be found under the File menu, in both the desktop and online versions. When all of the writing and editing, adding styles, images and urls is complete, students simply click on File, then Transform.

This method has one slight advantage over using "Start from a document" in Sway. Word Transform allows you to select a theme before the transformation to a webpage occurs. I say slight advantage because you can always edit both the content and the style in Sway after transforming it from a Word document, but it is convenient to select a style up front.

IMMERSIVE READER

35 Read Aloud

Immersive Reader is not just one tool. It is an entire suite of accessibility tools for reading. The core feature, read aloud, is hardly unique, but the fact that the read aloud is paired with so many other tools makes it incomparable, especially for a free tool. Immersive Reader, like many innovative tools in Microsoft Office/Office 365, began life in OneNote. Even though the general trend with Office is that the best tools are the desktop versions, and the online versions are more or less stripped down, Microsoft has reversed that trend for their accessibility tools. Immersive Reader is available full featured in OneNote Online and Word Online, meaning it can be used to its full potential on a Chromebook. You'll also find Immersive Reader in Word Desktop, OneNote App, and Minecraft, and now also in Forms. Although the text to speech is computer-generated, it is excellent at reading with inflection. There are settings for speed and a couple voices to choose from.

36 Line Focus

Everything about Immersive Reader is grounded in UDL- Universal Design for Learning. Each feature is available to absolutely everyone, and each can be turned on by an individual when they need it, and turned off when they don't. Another hallmark of UDL is that tools that were designed for

individuals with a disability are found to be useful for those without a disability. Line Focus exemplifies this truth really well. Line focus blacks out the entire screen except 1, 3 or 5 lines. The 1-line version highlights the line currently being read aloud. (The word currently being read is further highlighted.) The "spotlight" doesn't move down the page. Rather, the text is brought up to the spotlight. That means students don't need to visually track down the page. So, even though I often describe this as the digital version of holding a card or ruler under the line of text you are reading in a book, it's actually an improvement on that. The 3-line and 5-line can be used to wean off the line focus.

  Bonus tip: That bit about this being good for people who don't have a reading disability? Line focus also makes an excellent teleprompter for broadcasting morning announcements.

 37 Background Color

Background color. Sounds boring, doesn't it? How about some context? Have you ever seen a student put a colored transparency over the page they are reading? If you've ever wondered what that's all about, head over to http://irlen.org/ "Where the Science of Color Transforms Lives". Yes, science. They have decades of research about visual processing and factors that influence it, and for many people, color can be one of those factors. Immersive Reader provides both "dark mode" or "night mode" that you are probably familiar with from your phone, tablet or browser, and also a palette of background colors individuals can choose form to help with attention, comprehension and retention of written material. Once again, this digital version of colored overlays is an improvement on the physical version in that there are so many colors to choose from, and also because they are just one piece of this accessibility suite.

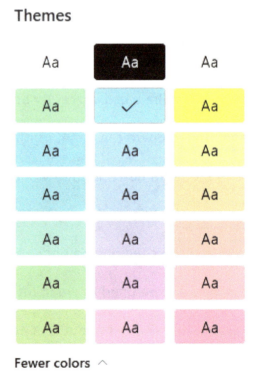

MICROSOFT STREAM

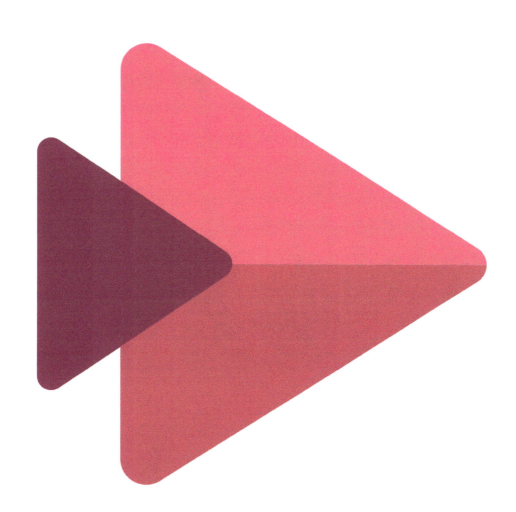

38 Upload Tutorials

Stream is one of the apps you can access from Office 365 by clicking on the App Launcher (the waffle). It is kind of like a private YouTube just for your school district. You can upload videos here and set permissions ranging from only individuals specified can view them, anyone in a particular group can see them, or your entire organization can see them, but nobody outside of your organization can view them, so there is a level of security. You can create Channels in stream, so you can organize your videos by topic, course or class. All videos auto-create an editable transcript on the right side that also functions as "click-to-go-to-this-part". When you use either the Slide recorder or the Screen Recorder in PowerPoint, they both give you the convenient option to upload directly to Stream.

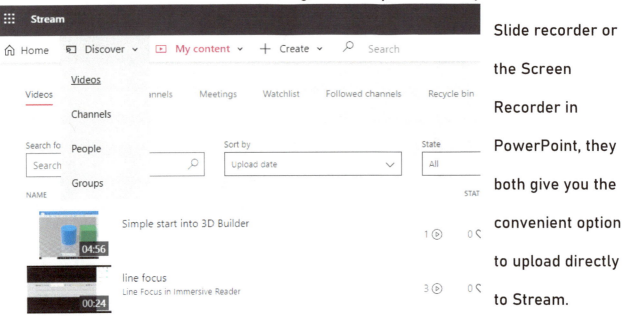

39 Upload Student Projects

Students get the same benefits in Stream. If they create a video, either with Slide Recorder or Screen recorder (or any other means of recording video) they can upload it to Stream as well. This works best for a class if the teacher creates a Group and adds all the students to that Group, then creates a Channel that is private to that Group. Students can then upload videos to Stream and add them to that Channel. That way only the teacher and students in that class can view that video. This also facilitates viewing for the teacher, since other videos from that channel will appear on the right of the screen to move from video to video. If more privacy is desired, the student can simply upload the video and choose to make it private and only viewable by specific individuals.

Stream has a new option that allows you to do a screen recording right within Stream, so you don't need to use PowerPoint or another screen recorder. Choose whether you want to add a web cam, whether you want to narrate with a microphone or include your computer's audio.

40 Captioning

One of the benefits of uploading your videos to Stream is the auto-generated Closed Captioning.

Having Closed Captioning obviously greatly enhances the accessibility of your videos. You also have some control of how those captions display on your screen when you access the video. So, by "you" I mean the viewer has that control. As you can see there are three font sizes, 4 color choices and you can turn transparency on or off. Transparency lets you see through the text, which becomes more important if you choose a larger text box but can also lead to reduced readability of the text when the background is the lightness/darkness as the text. Stream can currently produce Closed Captioning for English and Spanish. When you upload your videos you can indicate what language you are speaking in the video. In the future the plan is to support many additional languages, like PowerPoint captioning already does.

FLIPGRID

 41 Video Responses

An entirely different way to utilize video recording in the classroom is using Flipgrid. Microsoft bought Flipgrid in early 2018, gave everyone all of the paid features for free, and even gave refunds to individuals who had previously purchased the Pro plan. Flipgrid is web-based, so it can be used on any devices, including any smartphone. At its most basic, teachers post a question, either in text or by recording themselves asking the question and posting the video. Students respond to the question by recording themselves and posting their response. Flipgrid is designed to be a video conversation, so students can see each other's posts, but if more privacy is desired you can use a "moderated" mode so only the teacher sees the posted videos. Flipgrid has added a lot of features and some very creative teachers have come up with inventive uses for this simple video response tool.

 # 42 Advice for Next Year's Students

One of those creative ways to use Flipgrid is to have your students record advice for next year's students. Flipgrid becomes the platform for crowdsourcing your students' wisdom and like all things Flipgrid, is inclusive of those students who either have difficulty with written expression or simply prefer talking to writing. For those students that would actually prefer writing or are just camera shy, they can write out cards and hold them up to the camera.

Bonus tip: If you are looking to get your students to practice using Flipgrid or getting comfortable in front of a camera that's not affiliated with Instagram, click on Inspiration at the bottom of your screen and let Flipgrid provide the topic. Click on "New Inspiration" for additional ideas.

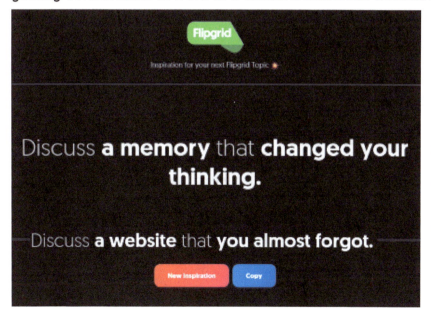

 43. Field Trips

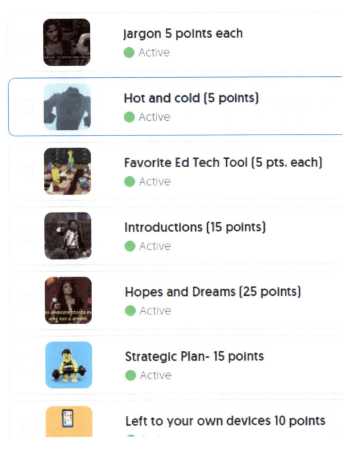

Another popular way to use Flipgrid is on field trips. On a typical field trip, students break up into small groups led by a chaperone and groups travel around mostly independent of each other, so by nature students don't all see the same things. Create a Grid in Flipgrid for the field trip and post different Topics on the Grid. (Think of a Grid as a class or an event, and Topics are the different questions or assignments the teacher creates within that Grid.) Mix up the easy "What was your favorite" question prompts with deeper ones like, "Which exhibit was most meaningful to you (or challenged your thinking) and what made it so?" It's easy to incorporate a Tic-Tac-Toe or menu format as well. Make questions worth differing point values and require students or teams to reach a certain number of points, with either more less challenging or fewer more challenging Topics.

 # 44. Sales Pitch

Another idea for using Flipgrid is to promote a product. Have students make a sales pitch. If it is a real product, shy students will appreciate that they can film the product while they narrate rather than their own face. This will involve planning, writing a script, collecting and organizing visuals, researching facts and data, all to create a persuasive presentation. However, this does not have to be an actual product. Have students record a sales pitch for an organism to highlight natural adaptations, or how multiplication is superior to mere addition, or turn an autobiography into a campaign advertisement.

Like Stream, Flipgrid now offers screen recording, and additional alternatives to students recording themselves on a webcam. They can choose to record a blackboard or whiteboard screen, or upload an existing video, or simply add a filter that pixelates the image. Accentuate the sales pitch by adding frames, stickers and text boxes. Flipgrid continues to innovate the video conversation with their ever-increasing editing tools.

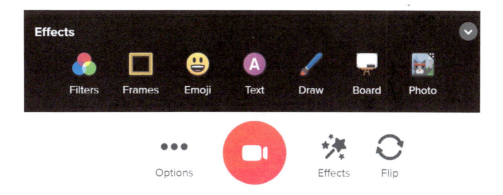

 45 Book Reviews

Another great application for Flipgrid is for students to complete book reviews. You can set up a Grid as an assignment for book reviews, or you can set  one up as a library of recommendations for students' favorite books. Or one grid could serve double-duty! Flipgrid now supports recording both webcam and screen-casting, so students can still stand in front of the camera, hold their book, talk about it, or act out a favorite scene. But now they can also create a PowerPoint about their book and narrate their recording of their screen, all from a web-based recorder, so it works on any device.

Regardless of which type of recording each student chooses, after recording they get to take a selfie for the thumbnail that people click on to see their video. Only, the selfie doesn't have to be a selfie. It can be a screen cap (Like pausing your video and taking a picture of that scene), uploaded image, or a picture of something else (like the cover of a book!) These are in addition to using the camera to take a selfie or other picture.

SKYPE IN THE CLASSROOM

 46. Mystery Skype

While Flipgrid is designed to be conversational but can be modified to use as one-way conversation, using Skype in the classroom is clearly a two-way communication tool. Skype in the Classroom is the difference between watching a movie and being in the movie. The easiest way to start using Skype is a Mystery Skype. Set up and account at education.Skype.com and search for other educators who indicate they are available when you want to connect. Or, Tweet out #MysterySkype with you preferred time and date. Once you set it up, Mystery Skype usually means playing 20 questions with another class somewhere in the world. The teachers know where each other are, but the students do not. Once you've played, you can continue the conversation or set up follow-up Skype events.

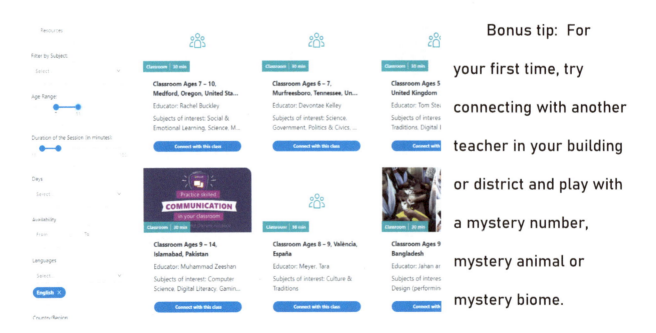

Bonus tip: For your first time, try connecting with another teacher in your building or district and play with a mystery number, mystery animal or mystery biome.

47. Virtual Field Trip

Another category of Skype connections you can make at under the Skype in the Classroom site (education.Skype.com) is Virtual Field Trips. Filter by subject, age group. Location, language, country and availability. Popular topics include Animals, Ecology & Conservation, and History & Culture. The website has a 1-hour course you can take to get more comfortable organizing it before, during and after the Skype session. Take you students to state and national parks, museums, monuments, coral reefs and more on any continent.

Geology Of Yellowstone

With over 10,000 mud pots, hot springs, geysers and steam vents, a supervolcano, and deep thundering canyons Yellowston...

Predators, NOT Pets

Turpentine Creek Wildlife Refuge is an accredited sanctuary and non-profit organization dedicated to resc...

Visit The VERKHOTURYE Museum In Russia

Visit the historical museum of Verkhoturye. The exhibition presents the history of the city and county Verkhoturye - the c...

Amazing Alligators! - NC Aquarium At Fort Fisher

Using live hatchling alligators, alligator artifacts, and fascinating

Mystery Skype With The National WWII Museum

The program will begin by revealing that your students are

Trappers, Traders, Trailblazers: Mountain Men Of The Rocky ...

Mountain men were rugged individuals who traveled,

 48 Author Skype

One of the most popular uses of Skype in the Classroom is to Skype with an author. The recently updated webpage, education.skype.com, makes it really easy to find authors to Skype with. Just type in "author" in the search box! The results include Guest Speaker session, Virtual Field Trips, Mystery Skypes and Collaborative Projects. That means your options are one-time connections and long-term projects, from detailed pre-determined lessons to open-ended sessions. Each author determines which formats they offer.

There are sessions with popular authors about their books and series, and others with authors about how to write, and occasionally large-scale events like the broadcast with Cressida Cowell, of How To Train Your Dragon. Fame.

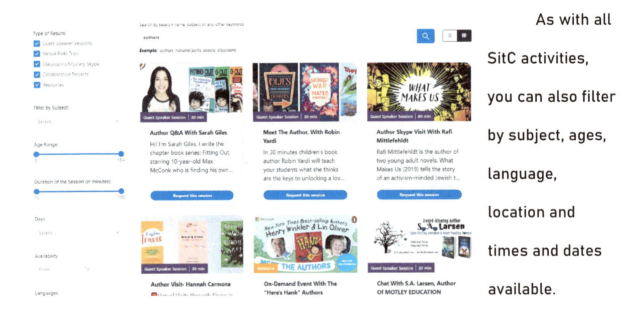

As with all SitC activities, you can also filter by subject, ages, language, location and times and dates available.

Before you run a session with any guest speakers, you'll want to plan with your students, determine roles, pre-select questions and go over netiquette.

ONENOTE

49. Digital Portfolio

OneNote has evolved to be many things. But in the beginning, it was a portfolio. I used to say you don't make things in OneNote. You put things in OneNote that you made somewhere else. (For safe-keeping, for organization) While that is no longer true- I use OneNote as a creation tool every day; I'm writing this book in OneNote- it still retains its place as a premier tool for student portfolios, but now with many more features and tools.

OneNote is a digital binder. It is a notebook, with divider tabs and pages within each of those sections. You can type anywhere on the page, and insert printouts of files anywhere on the page, resize and move whenever and wherever you need. Insert pictures, record audio, add weblinks, embed videos, use a stylus, touchscreen or mouse to draw with hundreds of colors of pens, pencils and highlighters.

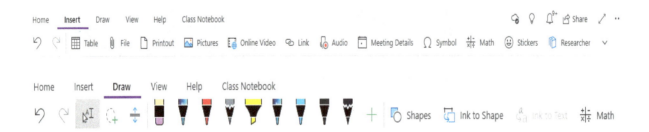

50. Print to OneNote 🖥️ 💻

Have you ever tried to print something, probably on a school computer, and accidently "printed" it only to have the computer ask you where you want to "save" it? Maybe it was "printing" to PDF, or Smart Notebook, or maybe to OneNote. There may be many options besides physical printers that you can print to. Printing to OneNote is one of the tools that makes OneNote so awesome for research and organization. You can be in Word or on a website in Chrome or Edge- anywhere that you can physically print something and choose OneNote as your printer". 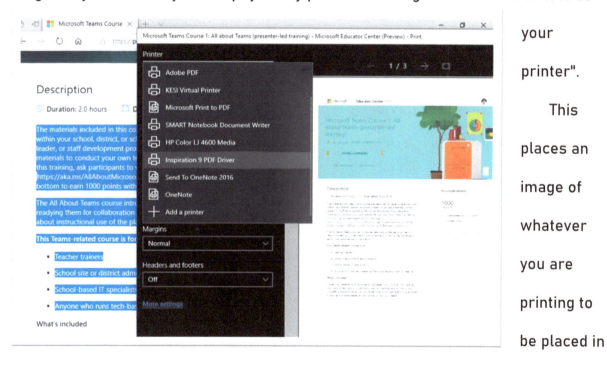 This places an image of whatever you are printing to be placed in OneNote. OneNote lets you select a new page in the section you currently have open, or print to the same page you have open, or search for anywhere in any Notebook to print to. So, no matter what you working on, wherever you are working, you can save it exactly where you want in OneNote.

51 Math Tools

OneNote has some really powerful Math tools. Type or handwrite an equation or a set of numbers and click on Math tools. Choose to view the solution or graph an equation, and show steps to solve the equation, and insert the graph or the solution steps onto your OneNote page. You can even choose to solve for x or y (or whatever variables you have.) For a set of numbers, you can find the Mean, median or mode, greatest common denominator or least common multiple, or even Standard Deviation. You can see the solution steps for these as well.

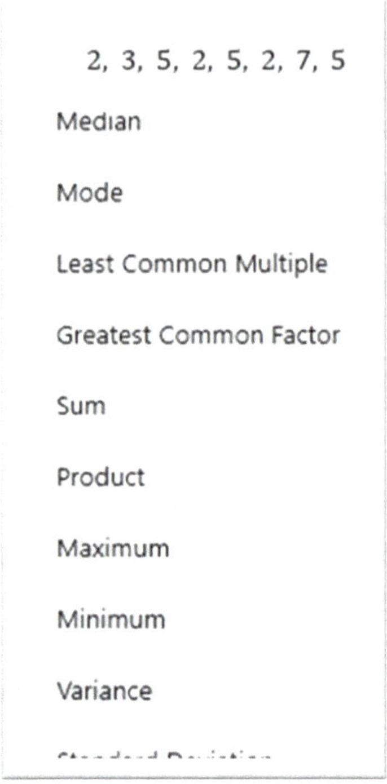

2, 3, 5, 2, 5, 2, 7, 5
Median
Mode
Least Common Multiple
Greatest Common Factor
Sum
Product
Maximum
Minimum
Variance

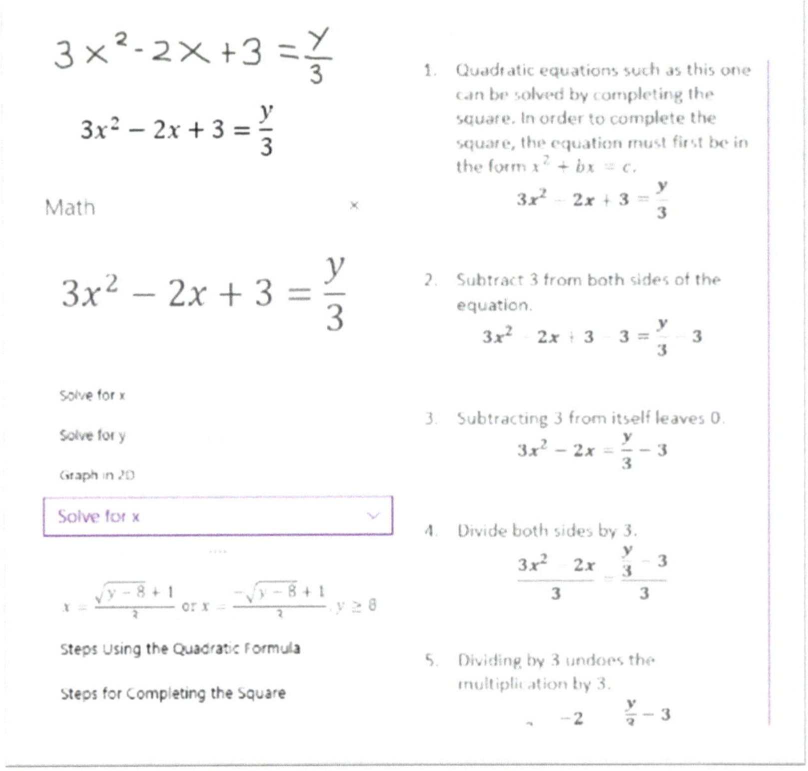

52 Ink Replay

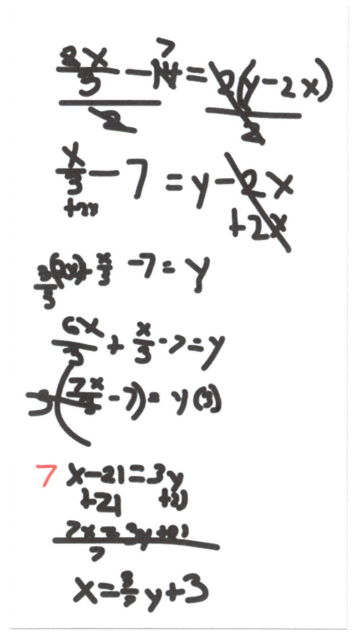

Ink replay is a nifty little tool that works with any inking you do in OneNote. Let's say you, the teacher, walk through solving this math problem live in front of your students in OneNote. You then share this page with your students. Each of your students can then use Ink Replay to watch every single ink stroke in order, pause, rewind and restart as much as they need. If you need audio, use the PowerPoint Screen Recorder instead, but for this video-only capture, the teacher doesn't even need to do anything- OneNote does all the work!

 53. Embed Sway

I keep reiterating that you can put anything into OneNote. You can be working inside of OneNote and reach out and grab things from other programs, or you can be in other programs, apps and websites and send things into OneNote. You can also embed creations within OneNote. Each Sway is a website, meaning it has its own url. Instead of adding the url to a Sway as a link in OneNote, you can embed the Sway so the Sway scrolls right on your OneNote page.

The link is live, meaning if you edit the Sway, you can see it updated in your OneNote as well.

54. Embed Wakelet

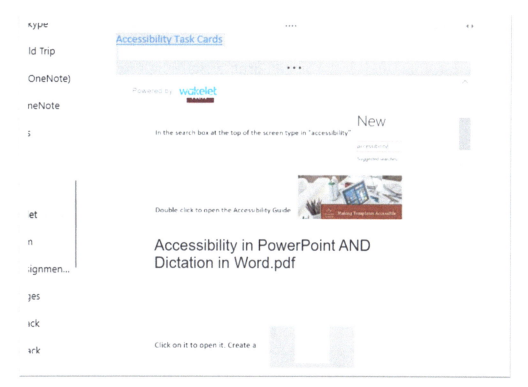

Another creation you can embed right within your OneNote page is a Wakelet. Although Wakelet is not a Microsoft product, a lot of Microsoft MIEs have fallen in love with Wakelet, which has facilitated some terrific integrations between Wakelet and several Office 365 apps. If you are not familiar with Wakelet, it is little bit like Pinterest or other modern Social Bookmarking sites, but also a bit like OneNote because you can upload documents, presentations, files and videos in addition to just weblinks. Wakelet is great for curating content. Most Wakelets are individually owned, but you can also make crowd-sourced Wakelets.

 55. Embed Stream

Returning to Office 365 integrations, another way to use Stream videos and channels is to embed them within OneNote. You can grab a share link to a video in Stream and paste it onto a page in OneNote and the video will play right on your page.

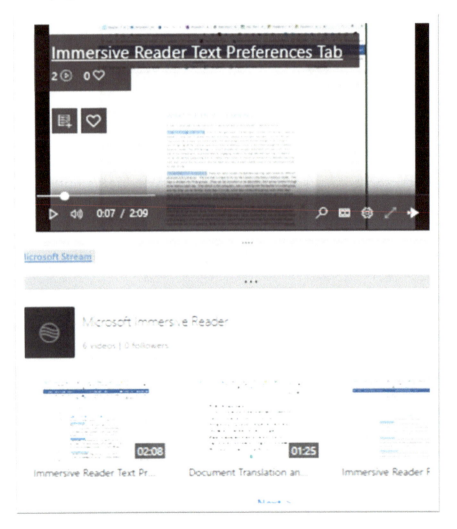

But you can also grab the share link to a channel and paste that in OneNote so students can click on any of the videos in that channel all from one convenient page! You can even turn on Closed Captioning or zoom to a specific part of the video by searching the transcript, right on the page in OneNote.

56 Office Lens to OneNote

Office Lens is available in both the App store for iPhones and the Play store for Android devices.

It has a number of functions. First, it takes pictures and straightens them out for you. Here's the same picture of a sign I took from the exact same spot, same angle, same distance, with my camera app, and with the Office Lens app.

Sign in camera app   *Sign in Office Lens*

Once you take the picture you can then send it to OneDrive, save as a PDF, or send the image directly into a OneNote, Word or PowerPoint, or share the image directly into Outlook or another email account you set up in Office Lens. But what's really powerful is the ability to share any image to Immersive Reader. Office lens is *handy* as a photo app, but it's *incredible* as an accessibility tool.

A student using Office Lens can open directly to full-featured Immersive Reader right on their phone. That means they can open *any text*, including textbooks, handouts, magazines and signs, and access all the reading accessibility tools of Immersive Reader, including read aloud and translation into 70 different languages!

A teacher can similarly send any image to OneNote and share the page with the entire class. OneNote uses OCR to open text from an image in Immersive Reader. Consider using Office Lens to not only digitize any paper handouts, and not only distribute them to all students by sending the image into OneNote and distributing through Class Notebook, but all students will receive a more accessible version!

This means students don't have to get up and move to a desktop, with all the related stigma, to have a device read aloud for them. They can stay at their desk, with their earbuds in, and nobody knows they aren't listening to music.

57 Insert Forms Quiz 🖥️ 💻

In addition to choosing to see the steps to solve the problem, AND open those solution steps in Immersive Reader to take advantage of all the reading tools there AND use the translation tools in Immersive Reader, you can also autogenerate a quiz.

Just type or draw a single math problem in OneNote. Use the select tool and "lasso" the equation. Select "Solve for x" or "Solve for y", and then a new option appears- "Generate a practice quiz".

OneNote begins talking to Microsoft Forms. When you click to generate the practice quiz, OneNote offers to create a quiz with 3 questions by default. You can choose anywhere from 1 to 20 questions. Microsoft uses machine learning (AI) to create a quiz with questions that similar to the one selected. Forms creates the questions, 4 answer choices, and an answer key and embeds in onto that OneNote page.

You can open the Quiz in Forms from One Drive.

$$2x^2 + 4x - 2y = -14$$

Solve for x

$x = \sqrt{y-6} - 1$ or $x = -\sqrt{y-6} - 1, y \geq 6$

You could then copy and paste the link anywhere for students to access the quiz (including Google Classroom if you are so inclined). In that case, students will take the quiz on Forms online and you will see their auto-graded results in Forms online as well.

Show steps

Generate a practice quiz

However, if you instead distribute the page that the quiz is on through OneNote Class Notebook, then students can record their work on the OneNote page, and submit answers to the Form directly inside of OneNote.

You will still see the auto-graded results in Forms, but also have access to their work in OneNote.

ONENOTE CLASS NOTEBOOK

58 Distribute Pages

In OneNote Class Notebook you can distribute pages. This is like the digital version of passing out papers, only much faster (with the click of a button) and with everybody's name already on their paper, and it distributes to absent students as well. In fact, the only way it's not better than physically handing out physical papers is that it won't help your step count. Simply go to any page in your OneNote Notebook and click on Distribute page under the Class Notebook tab in the ribbon. A dialogue box pops up so you can determine which section it will be added to in each student's OneNote Notebook for your class. You can now flip through and see each students' progress while they are working instead of having to wait until they turn it in. No more papers getting lost in bottomless backpacks or left on the kitchen table!

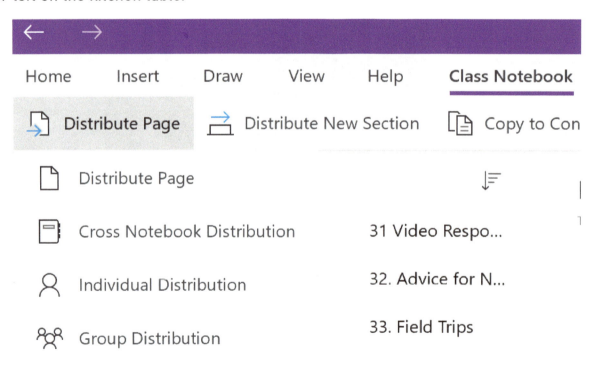

59 Distribute Assignments

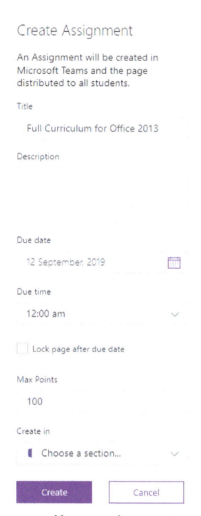

In addition to distributing pages in OneNote Class Notebook you can also distribute (among many other things) an assignment. This also places the assignment in each students' Notebook, giving them their own copy to edit. Creating assignments is available after you link your Class Notebook to your LMS or SIS, a one-time process that takes 2-3 minutes. Link to Microsoft Teams, or 3rd party products like Edmodo, Canvas, Moodle or PowerSchool. Why? Because assignments created and graded in OneNote Class Notebook can be automatically synced to your gradebooks in these platforms!

Your assignment can have a title and description and true due date- you can choose whether or not it locks after the date and time you select. Assign the point value, and choose what section in the students' notebooks to create the assignment in. If you are wondering where the content is, it's whatever page you are currently on in OneNote. Since a OneNote page is a limitless canvas, you can add any text, images, videos, links, documents and files your students will need. (You could say a OneNote page distributed as an assignment in Class Notebook is kind of what Hyperdocs want to be when they grow up!) It's that easy!

60 Teacher Only Section

The Teacher-Only section (actually section group) is a staging area for your content. As you complete your lesson planning throughout the school year you can add your content to the Teacher-Only section.

You can actually add other sections and section groups within the Teacher-Only section. In the example below, there are section groups within section groups (aka nesting), which you've probably done in OneDrive, Google Drive, or your hard drive using folders within folders for organization.

Feel free to work here without worrying about what it looks like or whether students can get in there and see it. (They can't.) This is your work space. The Teacher-Only section can actually hold your entire curriculum in your notebook. Some of it is literally for teachers only, and you will *never* share it with students. But the directions, rubrics, and student handouts are also in there. When it's time to distribute, depending on what content it is, I can send it to the Collaboration Space, the Content Library (for read-only, like directions) or distribute a copy to each student if it is for them to complete. Put this Notebook in Teams and get a bunch more options for distributing the content to your class.

61 Distribute to Students from the Teacher-Only section

When it is time to distribute material to students, click on the "Class Notebook" tab. If you want to share a single copy of read-only materials, like course matrials such as a syllabus, or reading selections, like an article, or directions, distribute into the Content Library.

Or, if you want to distribute a separate copy to each student to work on, edit, draw on or annotate, then distribute a page to one, all, or specific students in one class, or to all of the students in more than one class.

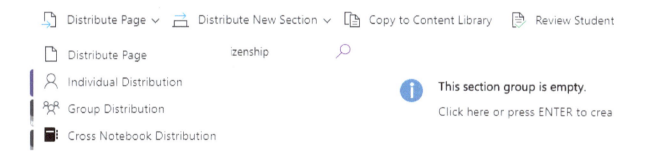

Again, if you create this Notebook as a Class Notebook inside of a Class Team, you get many additional options. You can access all the content in the Teacher-Only section to add as attachments to Assignments, to post as an attachment to a message, or add to the Files tab. I've placed the entire curriculum for a semester course in the Teacher-Only section in a Class Team and shared to both the Content Library and student sections as needed!

 62 Inking Feedback

When you use Class Notebook to distribute and collect assignments you have a variety of ways to respond to students. You can type or handwrite text, you can draw, circle, underline, annotate and highlight with the Ink tools under he Draw tab in the ribbon. Take advantage of OneNote's open, unlimited canvas to add inking anywhere, and combine with text boxes or audio comments for added effectiveness.

> This also places the assignment in each students' Notebook, giving them their own copy to edit. Creating assignments is available after you link your Class Notebook to your LMS or SIS, a one-time process that takes 2-3 minutes. Link to Microsoft Teams, or 3rd party products like Edmodo, Canvas, Moodle or PowerSchool. Why? Because assignments created and graded in OneNote Class Notebook can be automatically synced to your gradebooks in these platforms!
>
> *Why?*
>
> Your assignment can have a title and description and true due date- you can choose whether or not it locks after the date and time you select. Assign the point value, and choose what section in the students' notebooks to create the assignment in. If you are wondering where the content is, it's whatever page you are currently on in OneNote. Since a OneNote page is a limitless canvas, you can add any text, images, videos, links, documents and files your students will need. (You could say a OneNote page distributed as an assignment in Class Notebook is kind of what Hyperdocs want to be when they grow up!) It's that easy!
>
> *bold claim!*

Bonus tip: Try highlighting a snippet of student work, drawing an arrow from there to a text box where you type your contextualized feedback.

 63 Audio Feedback

Another way to provide student feedback is to insert audio comments. Whatever you would say if you were conferencing with the student 1:1, you can record. Click wherever you want to insert the audio comment. Combine your audio with inking. Chunk your audio comments by adding audio in multiple places- keep your comments in context! Students will be able to play the audio clips by just clicking on the icon.

or location and do the math to simulate movement.

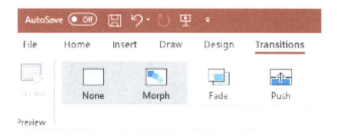

Which leads to the final product.
(Video)

Morph can show transitions visually, show order, processes, movement, growth and shrinking. Think about how you and your students can use this easy to use visual tool in your PowerPoint presentations.

23 Morph 36

Audio recording started: 2:46 PM Wednesday, September 11, 2019

MICROSOFT TEAMS

64 Use Teams to Communicate

There is so much to say about Microsoft teams, I don't know where to start. Microsoft Teams is the hub for all of the communication tools in Microsoft Office and Office 365. It combines Outlook's calendar, Planner's task management, Skype's video and audio conferencing, OneDrive's storage, the ability to share and collaborate on Word, Excel and PowerPoint files without leaving teams, all while reducing your email by using the chat and conversation tab in Teams. You can schedule meetings in Teams, have private a @Chat with individuals or groups, have a public conversation with the whole group, and share files in a shared SharePoint site. There's fun in teams, too. Try adding GIFs and stickers to your comments!

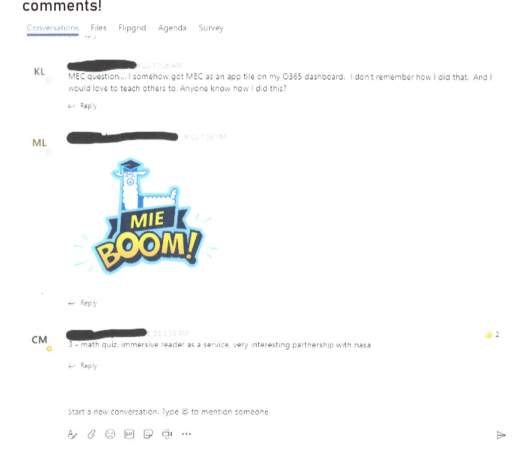

65 Conversation

The conversation tab in Microsoft Teams is a rich place. Obviously, you can type comments and messages to the Team. You can use @followed by a name so that person will receive a notification that they have a message. But you can also add attachments here, and when you add something to the File area, you can have it also appear in the Conversation area. You can add an attachment, emoji, stickers or GIFs, and post clickable web links. You can also reply to others and react with thumbs up or other icons.

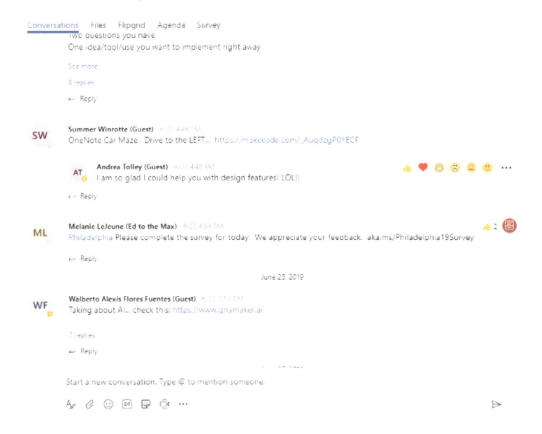

Not enough communication options for you? How about upgrading your conversation to a video meeting?

66 Video Meeting

Right in the Posts tab you can elevate your conversation to an audio or video meeting. Just click on the camera icon to schedule a meeting or meet right now. Don't want to be seen, only heard? Just don't click to turn on the camera. You can also share your screen with the other party (or allow them to share theirs), so this is also a good way to troubleshoot someone's device. Essentially, this is all the functionality of Skype for Business rolled into Teams. During your meeting use the chat feature to not only converse, but share web links and files, and give feeback and respond to each other's posts.Use the hnad-raise feature when youhave something to share with the whole group or need to ask a question without disruption.

115

67 Tabs

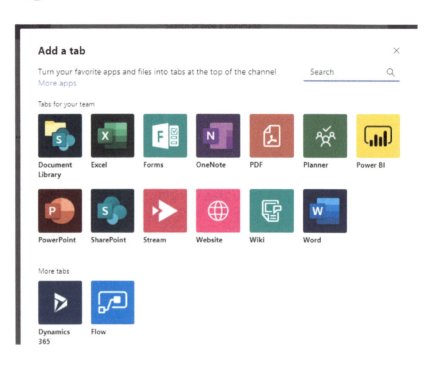

We've only touched on the Posts tab, but Teams is way more than just conversation posts. Teams also have a files tab which is a shared drive storage for everyone in the Team to share resources. Each Team type has its own OneNote Notebook- Class Notebook, Staff Notebook or OneNote Notebook. Team owners can add additional tabs like a Stream video or even an entire Stream library. Tabs can be temporary, so you teachers can add tabs for websites and documents to be used in class today for easy access and delete them when done with them. There are also tabs for Planner, Forms, a shared document library and 3rd party apps like Nearpod. Whatever you add in a tab, whether a file, app or website, it opens right inside of Teams, keeping everyone together in one collaborative learning space.

68 @ Mentions

Use teams to announcements. If team members turn on notifications in Teams, your messages will pop up in the bottom right corner of their computer screen even when Teams isn't open, just like Outlook. When people @message you, a red @ symbol appears over the chat icon on the left side-rail the "Me Space". Just click on it to see where your message is. Use @(name of team) to notify everyone of an important message. Since you can add attachments to your posts, this is a convenient way to distribute documents in the context of the message as well.

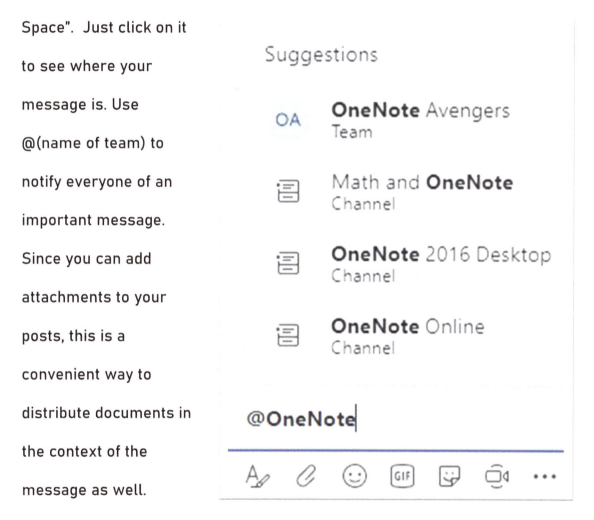

Because Teams is part of the larger Microsoft Office platform, you can also @ message groups that exist that were created in places like Outlook, or members of a private channel in a Team.

 69 Praise

Who couldn't do with a little more positive reinforcement? Teams makes it so easy. In addition to the other icons for adding things like a GIF to your comments, click on the ellipses (...) and you will find Praise.

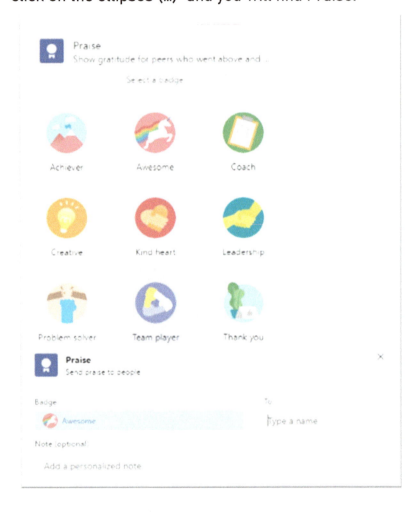

Just select a badge, add an optional personal note, enter the user you want to publicly praise, and it gets added to the conversation! Teams makes it so easy, you have no excuse for not spreading a little love. Do you have a shy student that you still want to acknowledge? Click on the Chat icon on the far-right in Teams. (The "Me-space) and start a chat with that student. Use the Praise option here and only that student will see it. This Chat area is for private chats. Chats anywhere eot the right in Teams, whether in a channel or a meeting, are viewable by everyone on the Team, even if you @mention an individual.

118

70 Assignments in Teams

Teams is your all in one digital classroom solution, which means it's a great platform for assigning, collecting and grading work. Assignments in Teams allow you to add directions, attachments, rubrics, and hard and soft due dates.

You can add directions right in the post, but if they are longer, you can put them in a Word document and attach it as a view-only document. You can also add a Word, PowerPoint or Excel file that creates a copy for each student to work on.

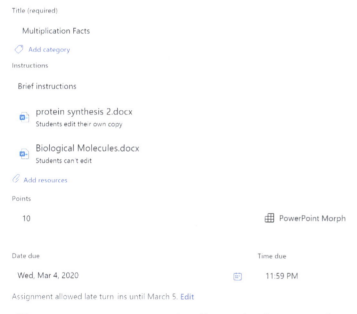

Create a rubric in Teams and it saves and is reusable on future assignments. You can grade directly on the rubric and the grade transfers to the gradebook. (Yes, Teams has a gradebook!) You can set a due date, and unlike Google Classroom, you can actually make it so students can't turn it in after the due date.

When you finish creating your assignment, you assign it to a whole class, to everyone in multiple classes, or choose individuals or small groups to assign it to in one class. Once you create those small groups, Teams remembers them, so you don't have to select those students again for the next assignment, another feature unique to Teams.

71 Reuse Assignments and Quizzes

You don't always need to reinvent the wheel. Once you create a rubric in Microsoft Teams, you can save it to reuse it with new assignments. The same is true for entire assignments. Once you have done all the work to create an assignment you like, you can reuse it. There are a few different scenarios for this. While you can choose to send an assignment to select individuals, or to multiple classes, you can't do both at the same time. So if you want to assign it to specific students in one class, you can. The to send it to select students in another class, you can reuse the assignment and assign it to individuals or groups in another class.

Another use is to reuse assignments from semester to semester or even year to year. When you select "From existing" you first choose which class to reuse it from (even the same class.) Why reuse an assignment in the same class? Because you can modify them. It makes an exact copy of the directions and attachments, points and rubrics. But if you want to modify anything, you can. So you can essentially create a template with directions, rubric and points, but swap out the content (the attachments)!

72 Different Due Dates and Deadlines

Assignments in Teams can have due dates. They can also have deadlines. Those can be the same or different. Does that sound confusing?

When you set a Due Date for an assignment in Teams, students see that due date when they open the assignment. If they click on their calendar, they will see the assignment posted at the due date (and time). However, that is just a "soft" target. Students can still turn the assignment in after that time, unless you check the box disallowing that. If you do, it becomes a "hard" deadline. But, those don't have to be the same date and time!

Date due

Tue, Mar 10, 2020

Assignment allowed late turn-ins until March 11. Edit

You can set a separate public due date, but also build in a grace period and set a hard deadline some hours or days after the due date. In fact, if a student contacts you with a convincing sob story and you want to let them turn it in after the firm deadline, you can (temporarily?) change the deadline to allow that, without altering the public due date!

PLANNER

73 Track Long-term Projects

Planner can be added to a team or used stand alone. You'll find it under the waffle (app-launcher) in Office 365. Planner is project management for individuals or groups. Create "buckets" like "To Done", "Assigned", "in process" "Completed", "Verified". These are completely customizable and you can have as many or as few as you want. Create tasks, assign due dates, and assign them to one or more people. You can add people up front or add them as you assign tasks to them. They will be notified in Outlook (or Teams) that they have a task assigned to them. This sample is set up so the "buckets" (columns) are tasks assigned to each person.

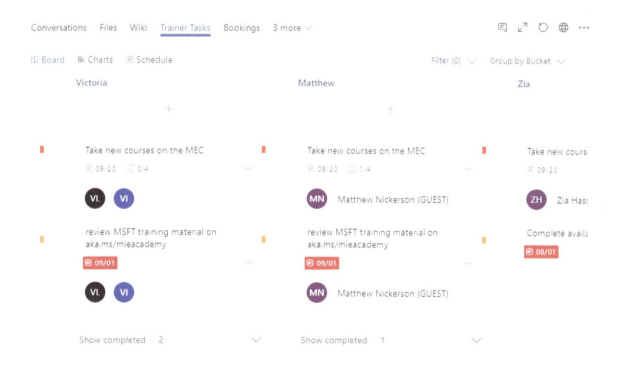

Bonus tip: Show students how to use this and they can enter all the steps for completing a long-term or research project!

74 Event Planning

Planner isn't just for student use. Use Planner with staff to plan events, trainings, or unit plans. I've used Planner for committees and to plan a Teacher-led conference. Planner makes it easy to see who is responsible for each task, and how far along they are in reaching those goals. There are several views to toggle between in addition to the bucket-view, like charts showing completion rates or a calendar of due dates.

BOOKINGS

75 Schedule Meetings

Bookings is another app you can find under the waffle (app launcher) in Office 365. It is a scheduling app. Your first Booking page connects to your own Outlook calendar, showing your availability. You can create "services" of varying lengths of time so people can schedule to meet with you whenever that size block of time is not filled in your calendar. Set up Services of 30, 60 or 90 minutes, 1/2 day and full day. When people select a service and a date on your calendar, they will only see availability of at least that length of time. You will both receive a notice in Outlook of the appointment.

Conclusion

My original title was going to be 365 Ideas for Office for Office 365, Volume 1. Then I did some math and realized it would take 5 volumes to hit 365 ideas at this rate. That title came from my blog series of the same name. I don't blog very day, so it's been just over a year and I just posted idea #100, so I'll be at that for a while. You can follow my progress at https://TheOther-IT.com I currently have 290 ideas, but Microsoft keeps adding new features so I'm confident there will be 365 by the time I get there. The point of this rambling on about numbers is simply to point out that the ideas contained in this volume are just the tip of the iceberg. Most of what you have read about and, hopefully, tried out, focused on individual applications, but I tried to include some examples of how these tools integrate so well together. That's one of the powers of digital tools, that their usefulness expands exponentially when you find ways to use them together. Just today I was sitting in on the first day of a two-day MIE Trainer Academy, and someone asked how to use the MEC (more on that below) so create a workflow of courses for their teachers to train themselves. Since we had already been introduced to Wakelet that morning, I pointed out that they could curate the list of courses they recommend for their teachers on Wakelet. Sway would work just as well. Using one digital platform to facilitate learning others.

As I mentioned, one resource for continuing your implementation of Office 365 in your classroom is my blog, The Other-IT. (BTW, that's Instructional Technology, as opposed to Information Technology.) A more formal, more structured, and larger resource is the MEC, The Microsoft Educator Community, found at https://Education.Microsoft.com This site is filled with training materials, webinars, videos, and courses that also feature digital badging to document your learning. The MEC is also a community with forums where you can ask question and share ideas with other educators. If you conduct training, you'll also find complete training packages for trainer-led sessions, typically a OneNote for the course with instructions for the presenter and a matching PowerPoint slide deck. You'll also find information about applying to be part of the MIE Expert program. Make sure to create an account and start earning your badges! Skype in the Classroom is now its own separate site, https://education.skype.com. Rounding out these teacher resources is https://education.minecraft.net.

I'd love to see how you use these ideas, and the creative ways that you have found to make learning more accessible, more engaging, more collaborative, in short, more effective with Microsoft Office 365. You can do that by tweeting them and including @dadxeight (Yes, I have 8 children. Thank you buying my book!)

If you are interested in Microsoft Education in person training for your school or district, consider contacting an Microsoft Training Partner like i2e, (Insight2Execution) http://www.i2e-llc.com